COLOR ME NOW!
...1...2...3

THE BEAUTIFUL PIN-UP GIRLS
OF THE 1940'S-1950'S

BY RACHEL GANZ

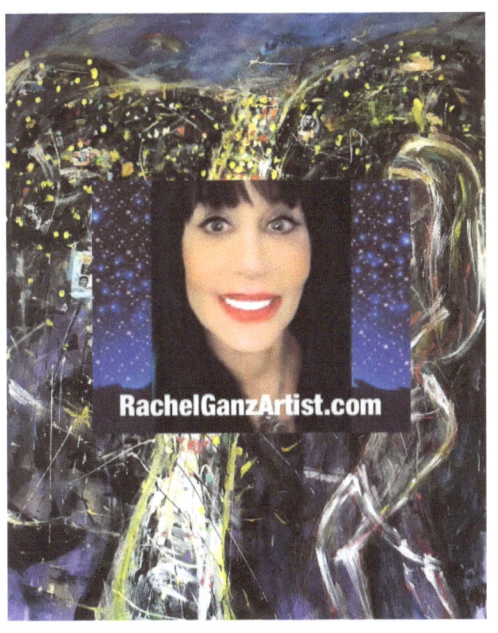

RachelGanzArtist.com

WWW.RACHELGANZARTIST.COM

Dedication

This book is dedicated to my mother "Florence Wigder Seltzer", (devoted wife, mother, grandmother, school teacher & speech therapist) and to all 'Mothers' as we are nurturing, kind, forgiving and strong

I chose the 1940's-1950's period of time, as women were all radiant beauties without Botox or plastic surgery. These natural beauties were happy and content in their defined roles as mothers and house-wives, who stayed home to raise their babies.

Post World War2 was a time of peace and contentment. Almost anyone could afford to buy a house and live the "American Dream".

"Color Me Now! 1.2.3 The Beautiful Pin-Up Girls Of The 1940's-1950's" is a lively coloring book to escape to an era that was peaceful, natural, fulfilling, and fun! Be creative use your colored pencils, pens, crayons and paints and let it flow.

This book is a tribute to my mother, your mother or grandmother…to all Mothers present or past.

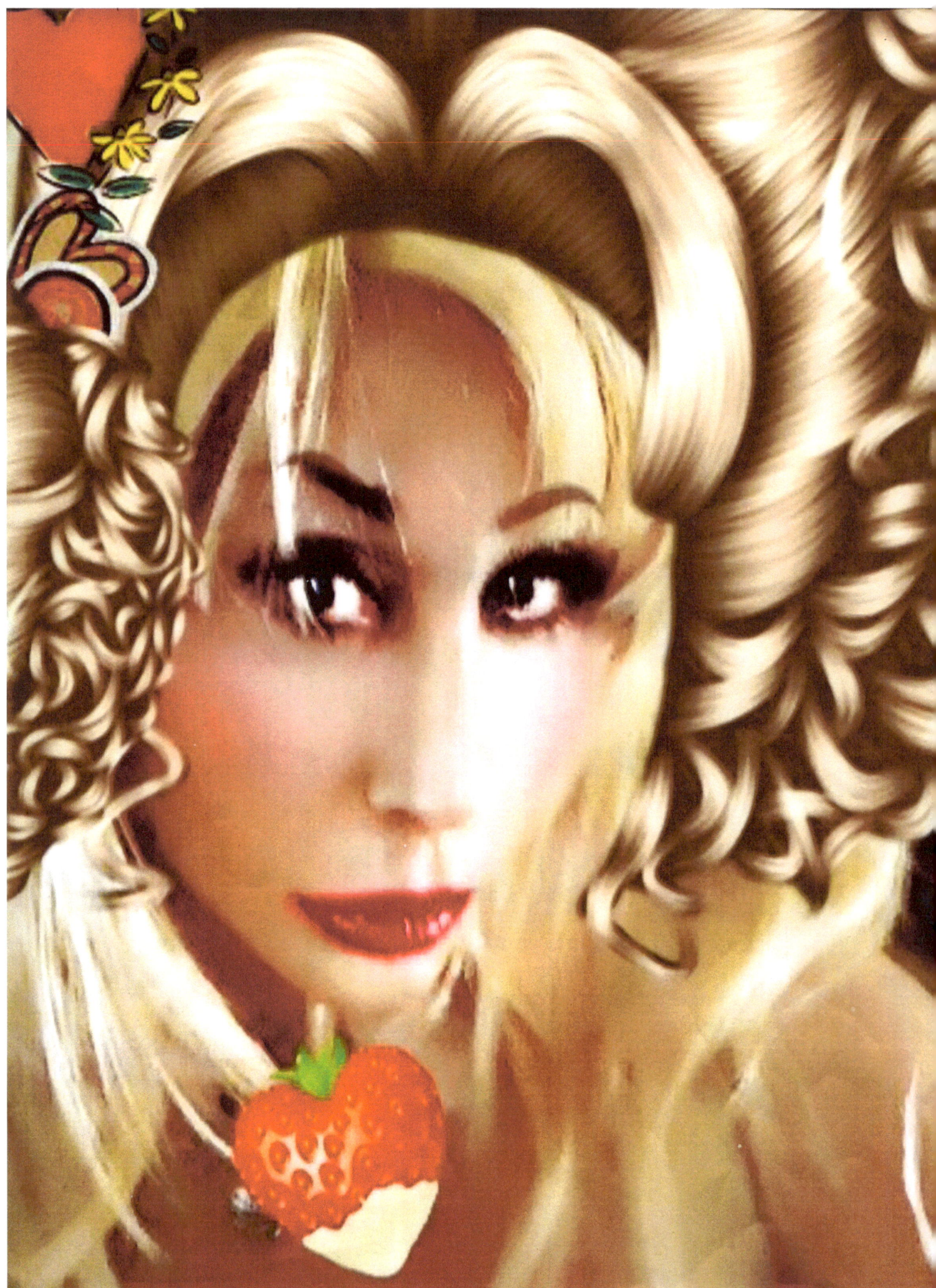

Biography

My name is Rachel Ganz

I've been selling and exhibiting my art privately throughout the United States and Europe. I have been fortunate enough to have patronage that appreciates my talent

I owned, opened, and directed my first and only art gallery from 1996-1999, La Mermaid Galerie' D'Art , 323 Worth Avenue, Palm Beach Florida

During the time of my art gallery, I donated many original pieces of my art to benefit numerous charitable organizations

I am currently residing in Los Angeles where I do some freelance entertainment writing and sell my art privately My new website "RachelGanzArtist.com" Is under construction and should be functioning soon

I hope my adult coloring book " Color Me Now! 1..2.. 3. The Beautiful Pin-Up Girls of the 1940's-1950's" will bring you joy and pleasure in coloring my playful figures as well as exposure to an era that is past but should not be forgotten!

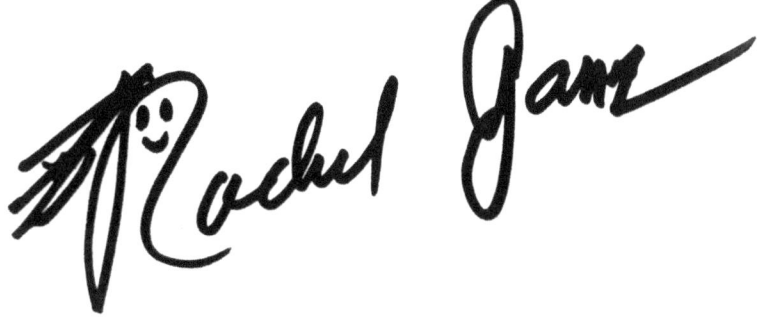

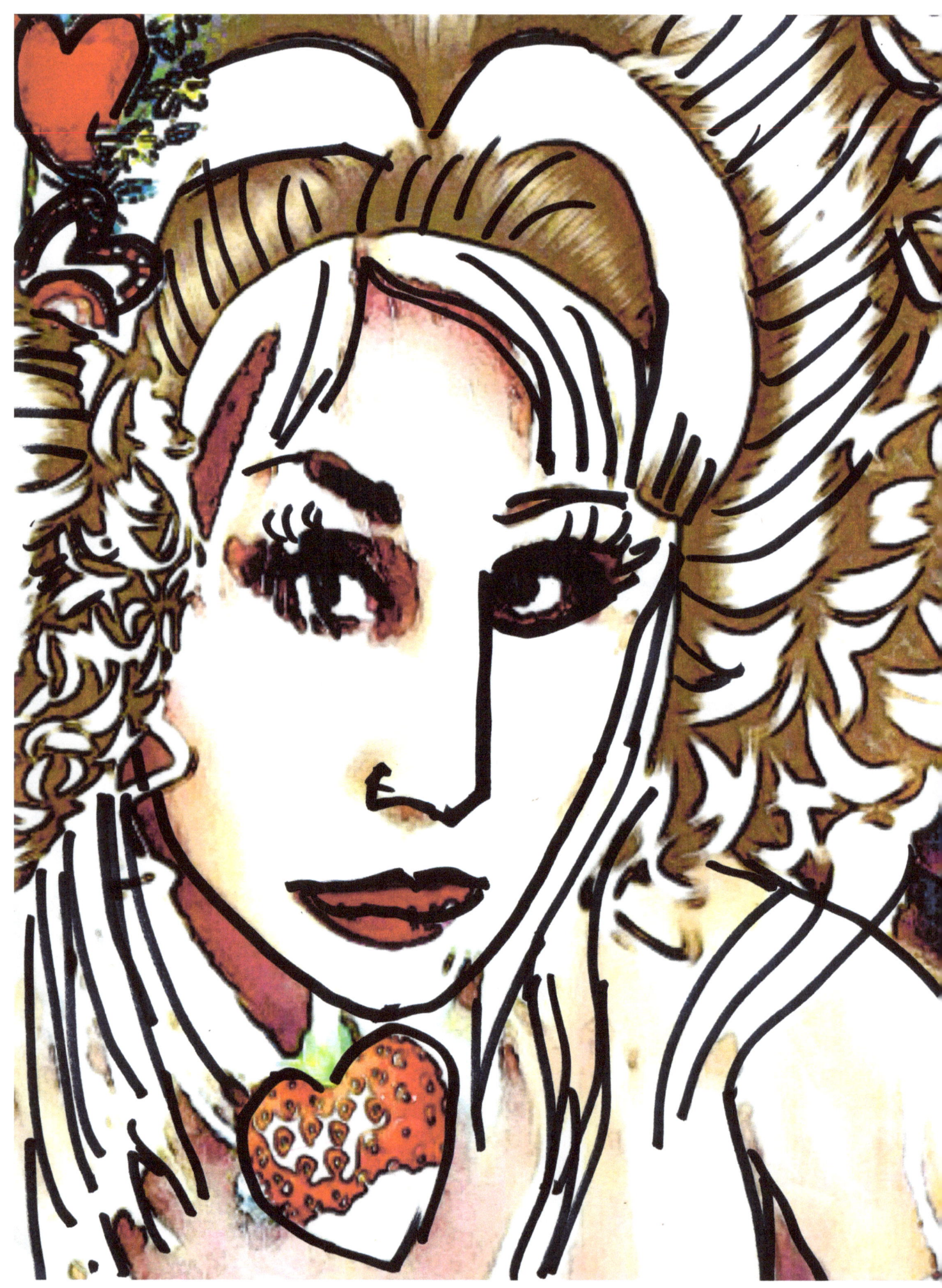

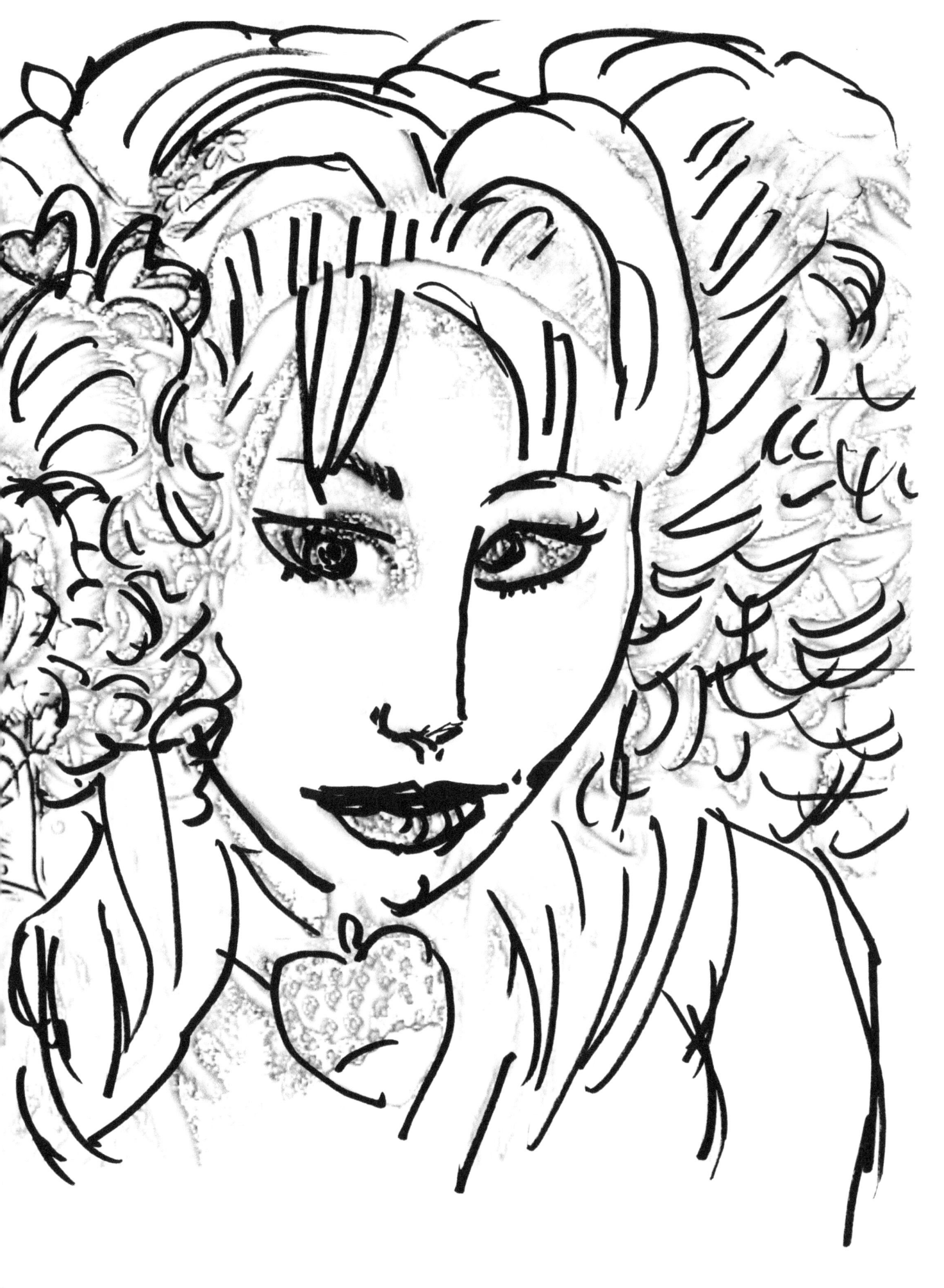

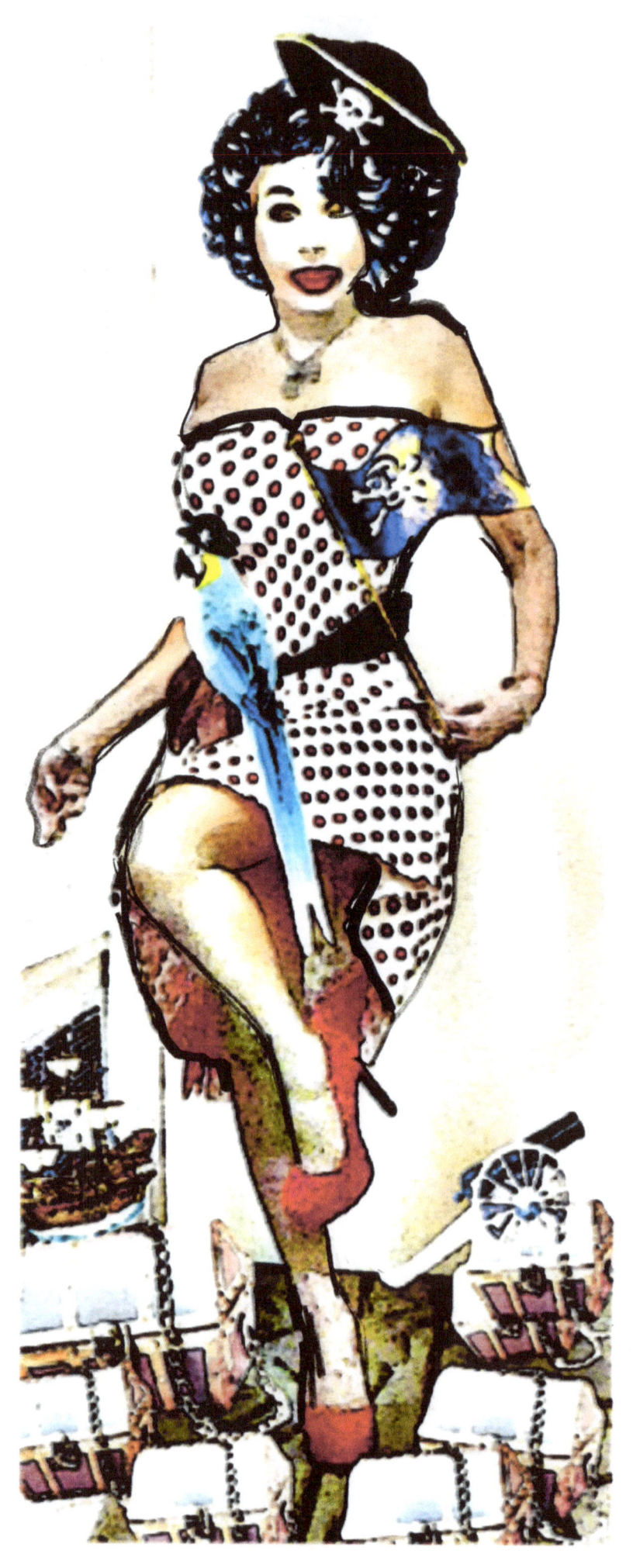

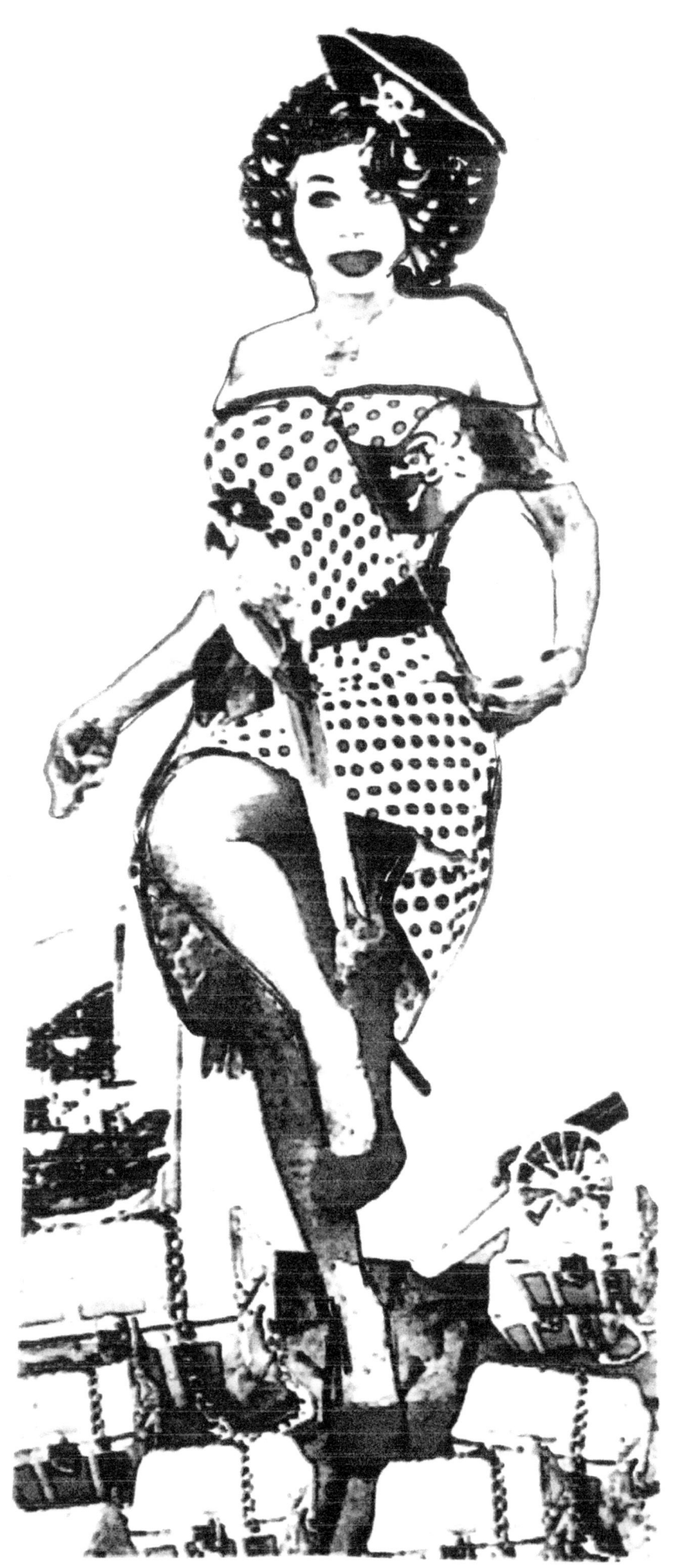

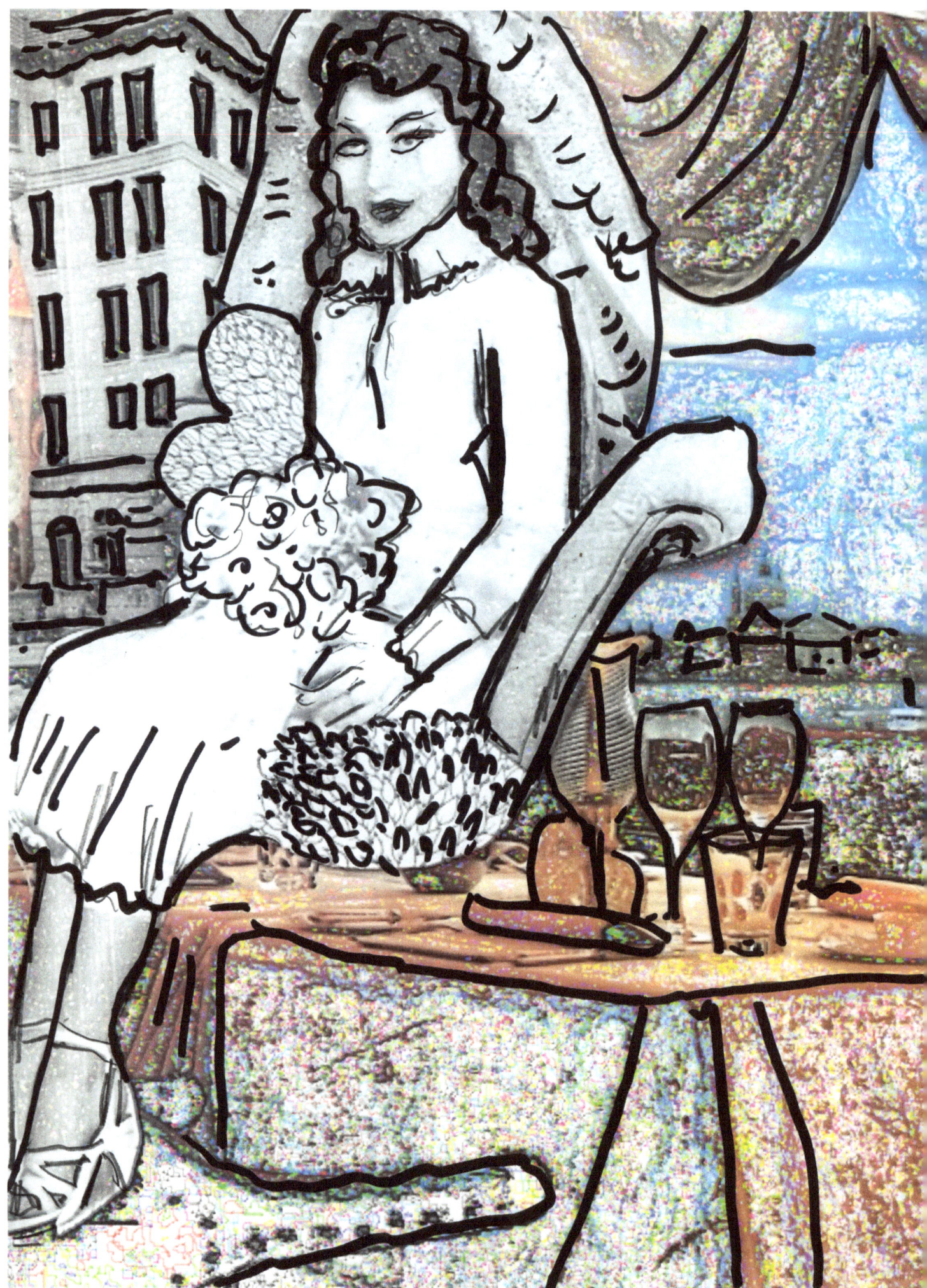

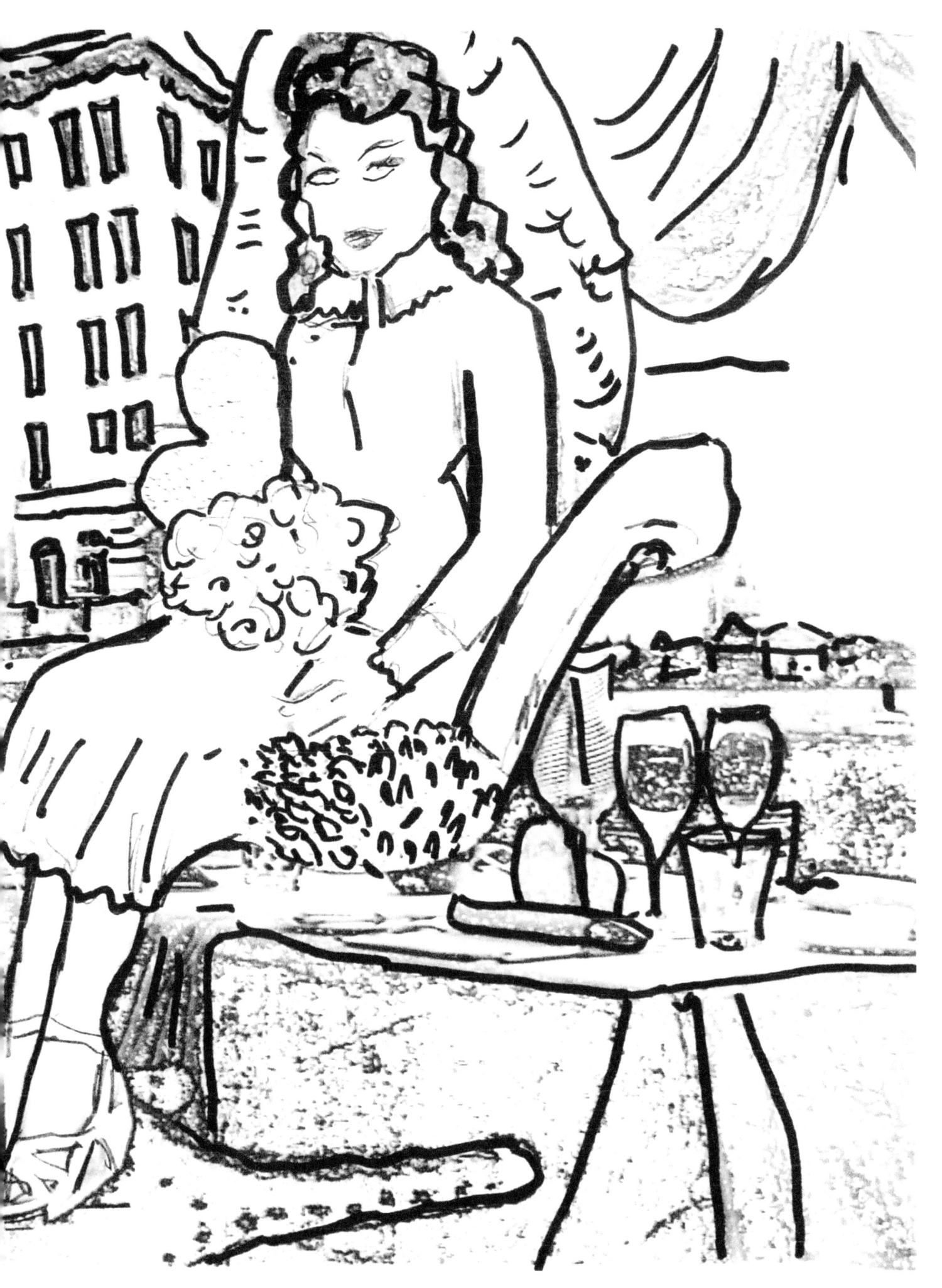

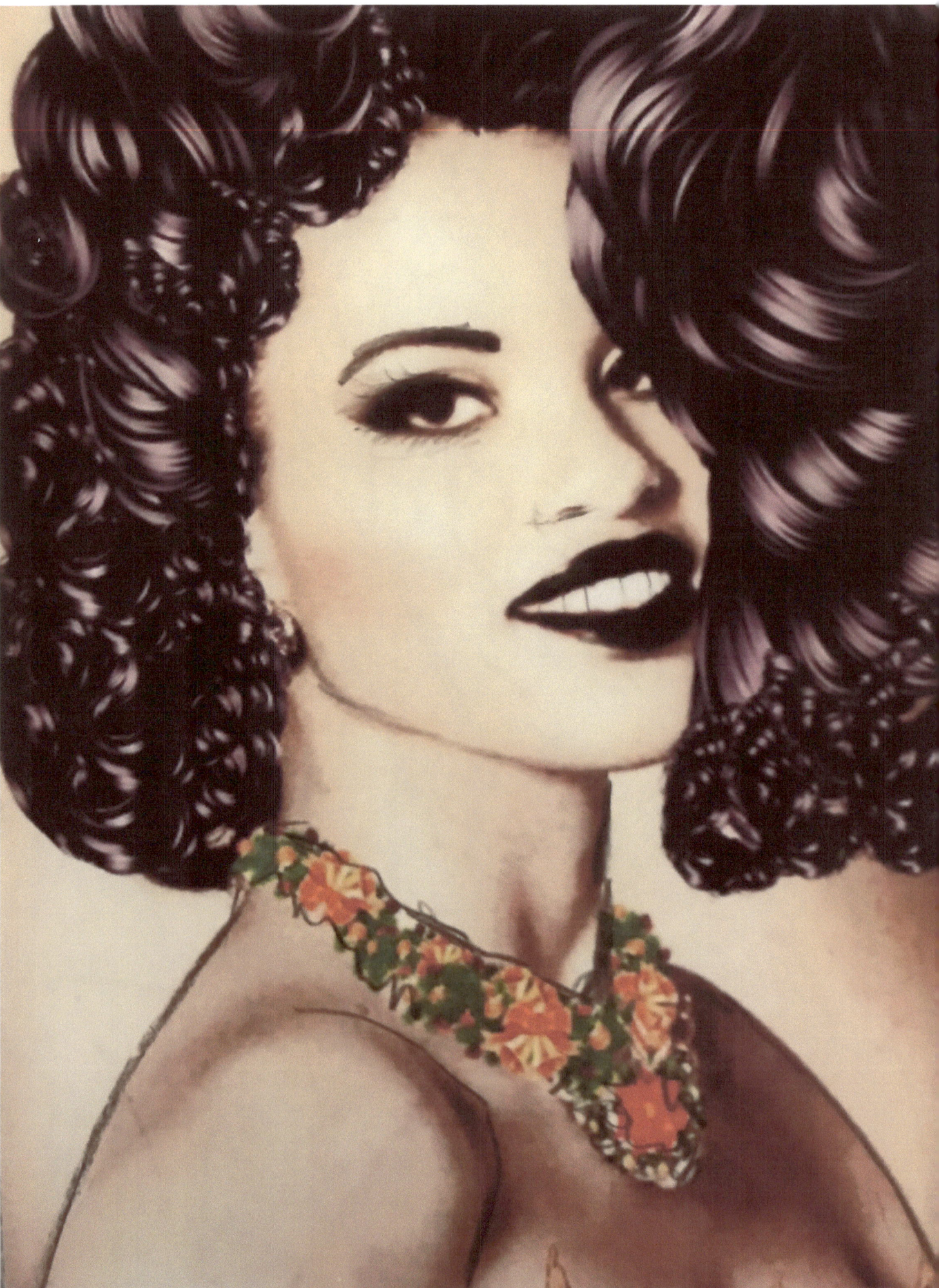

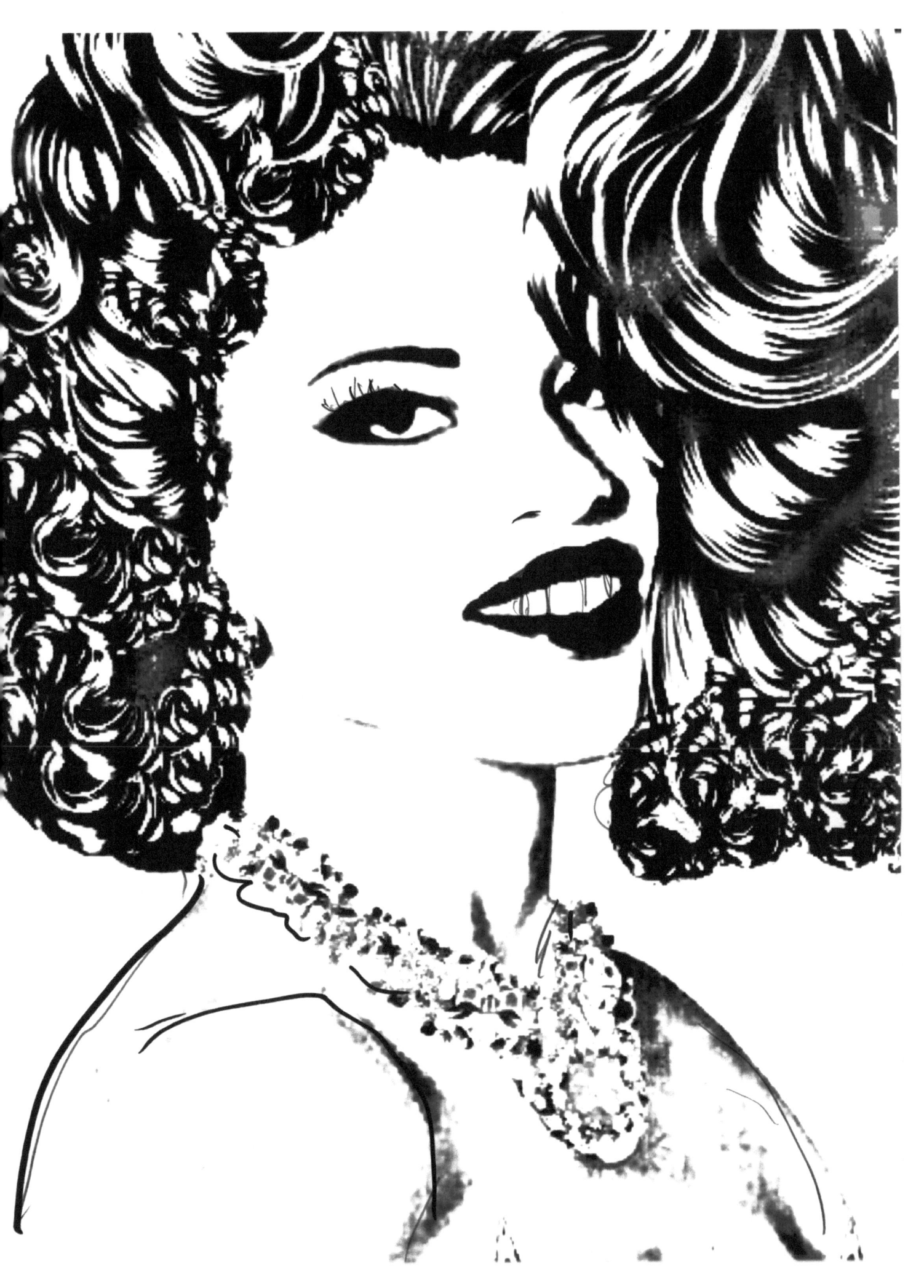

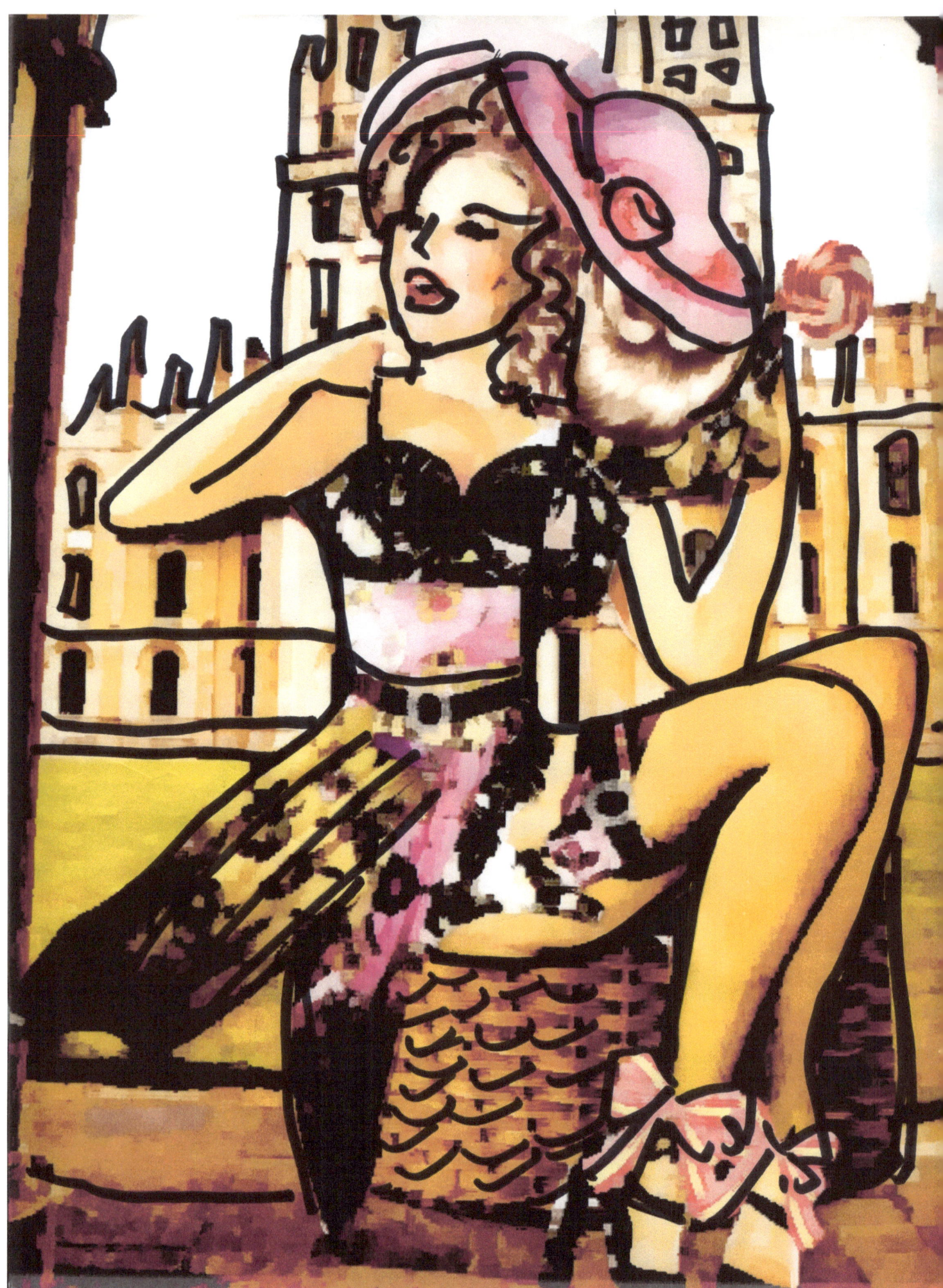

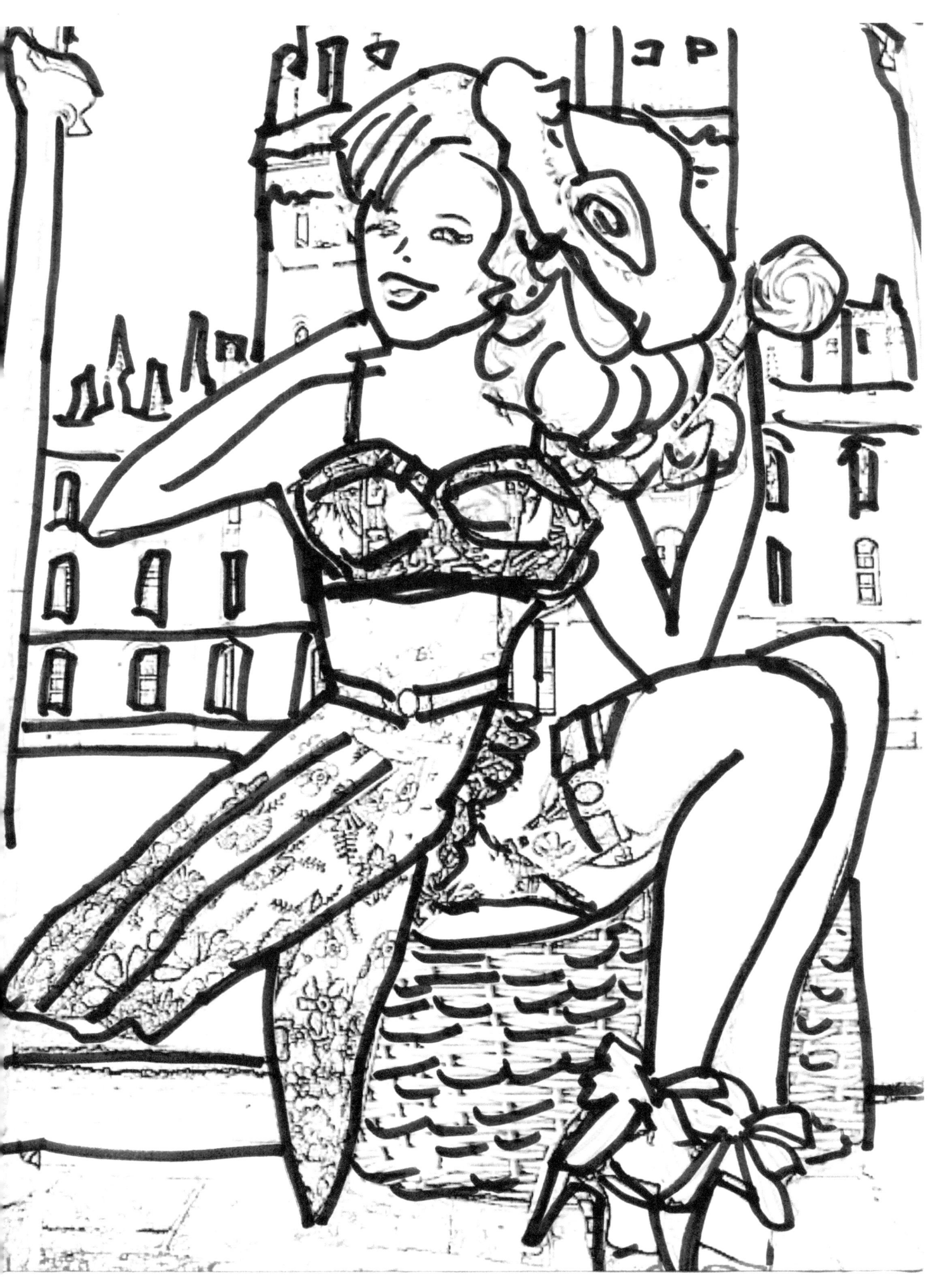

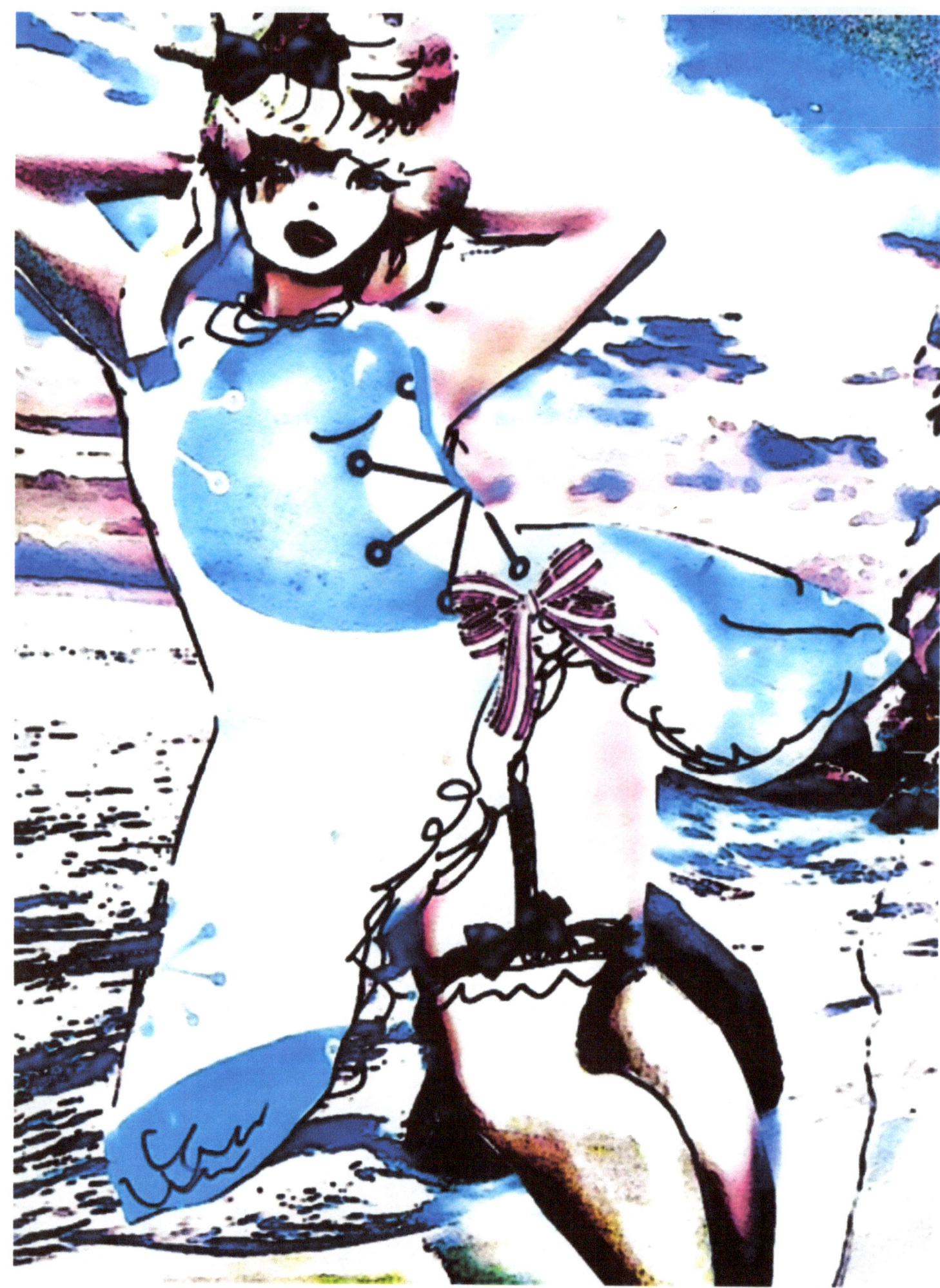

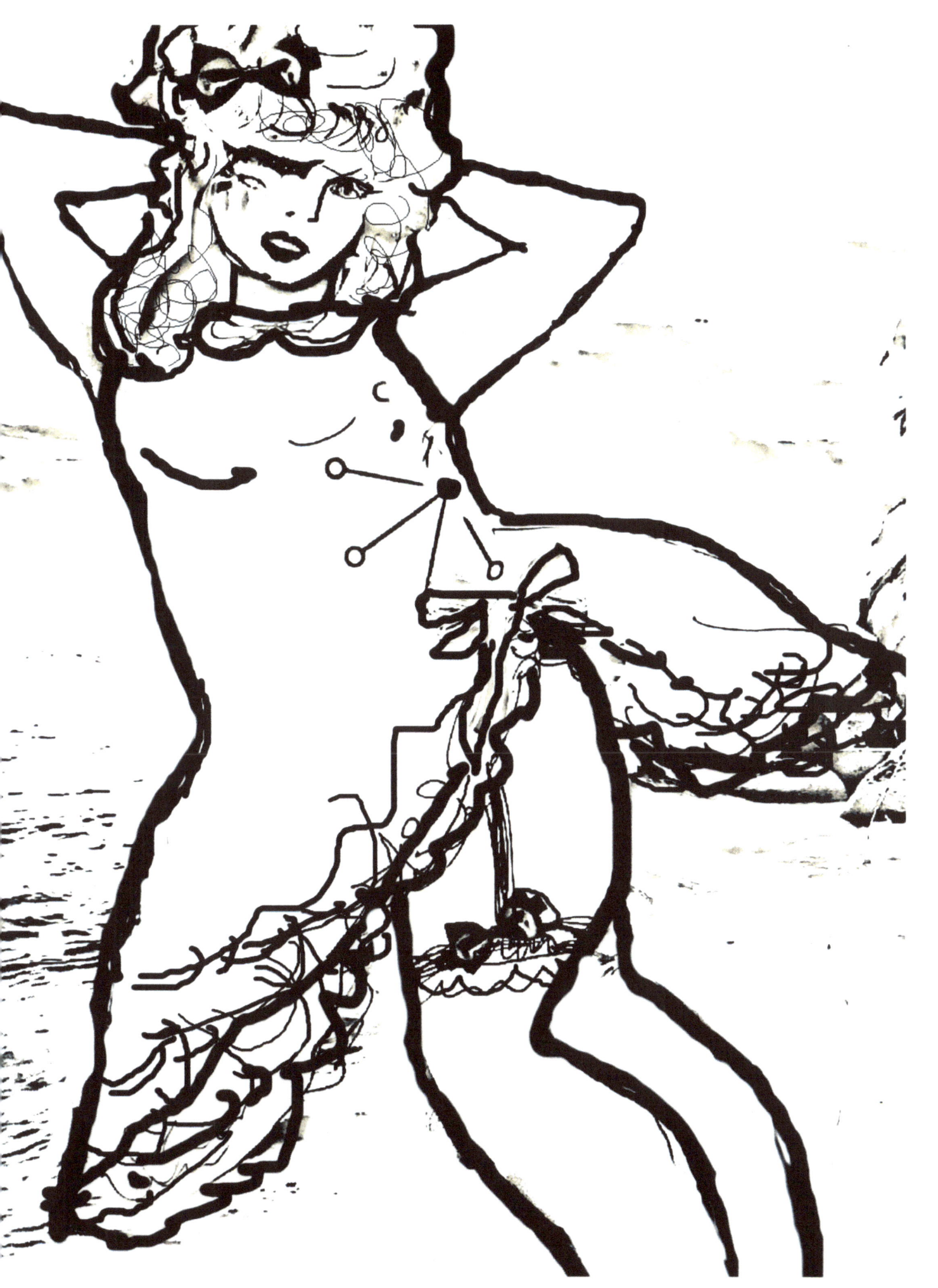

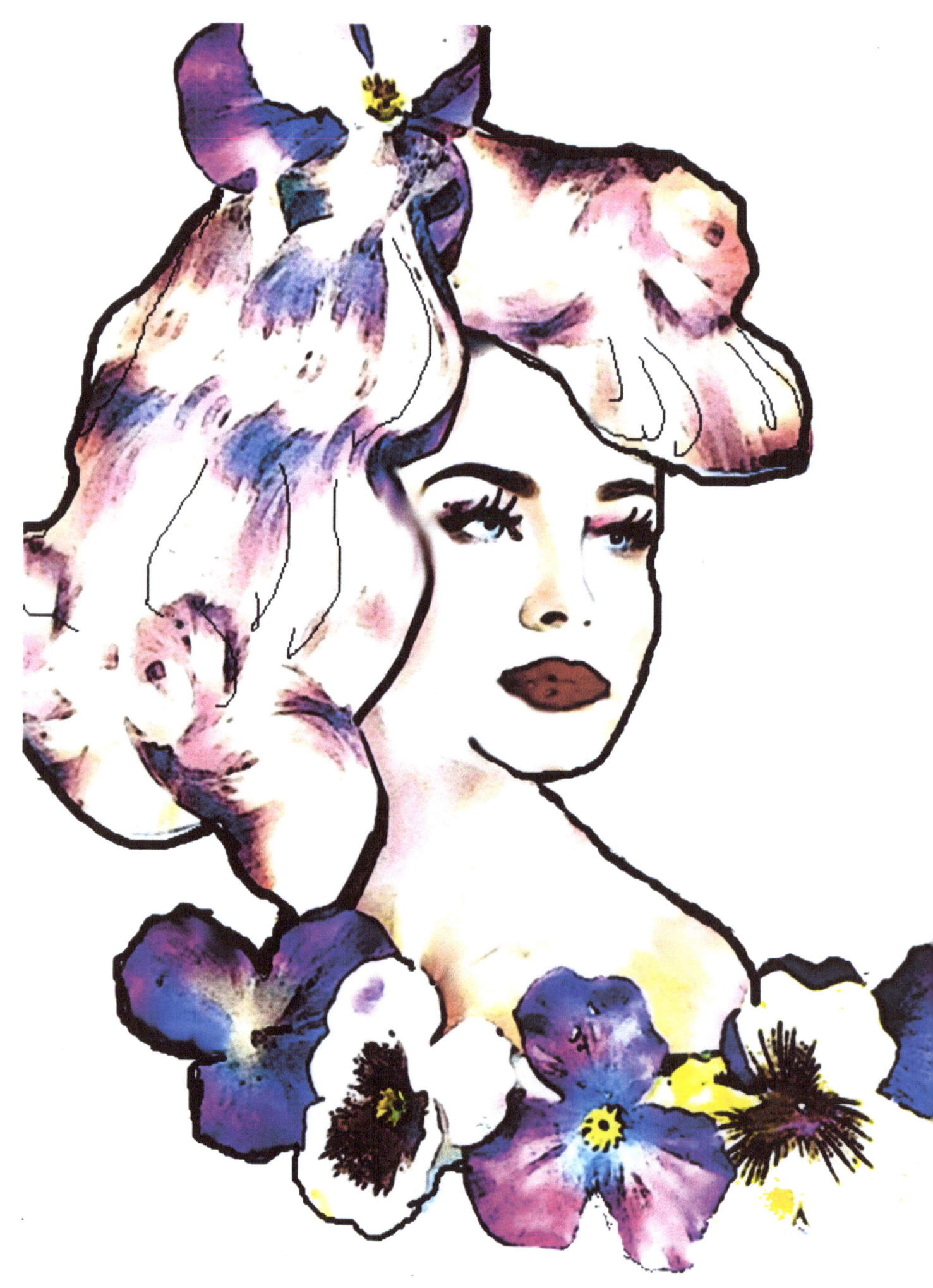

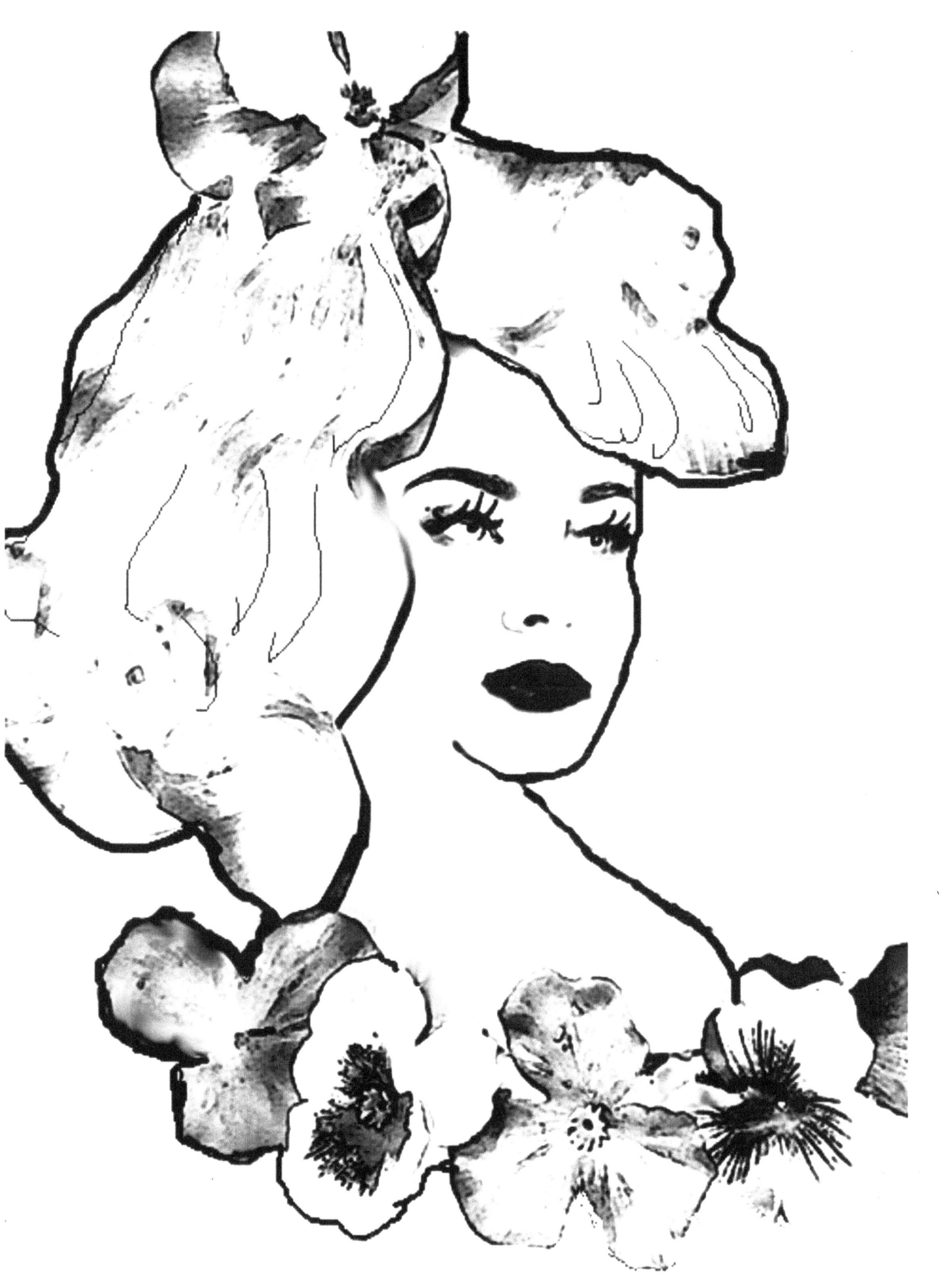

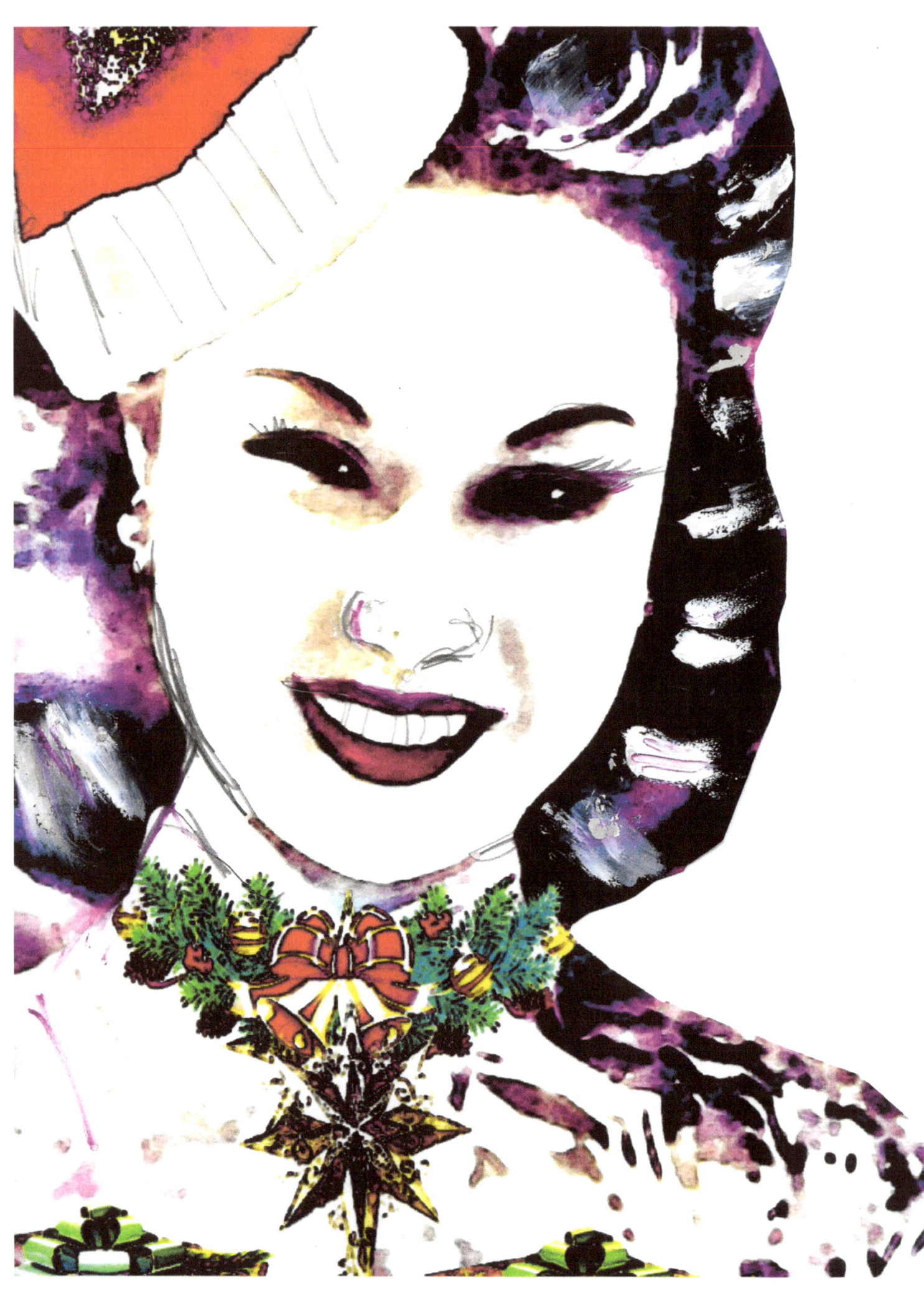

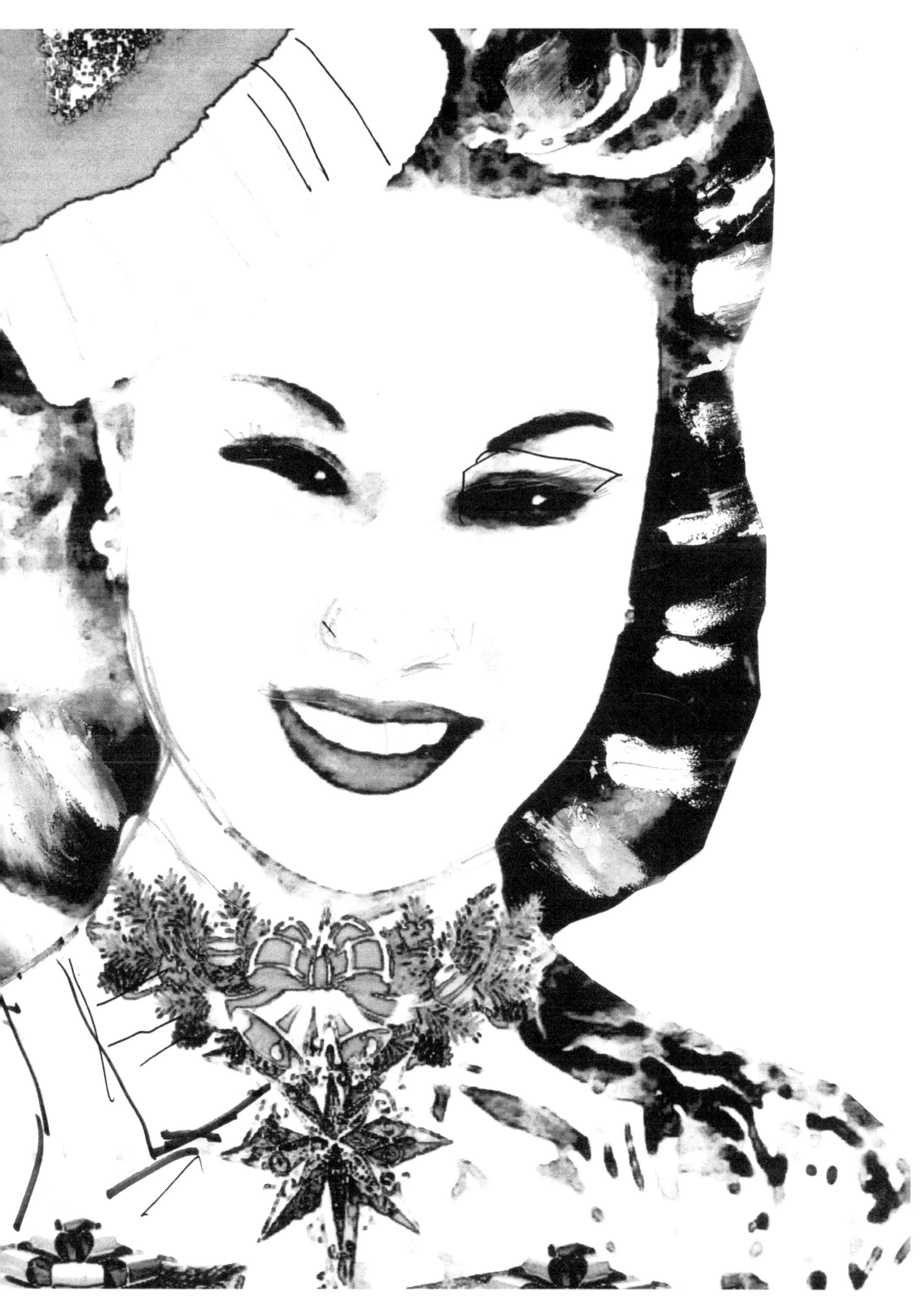

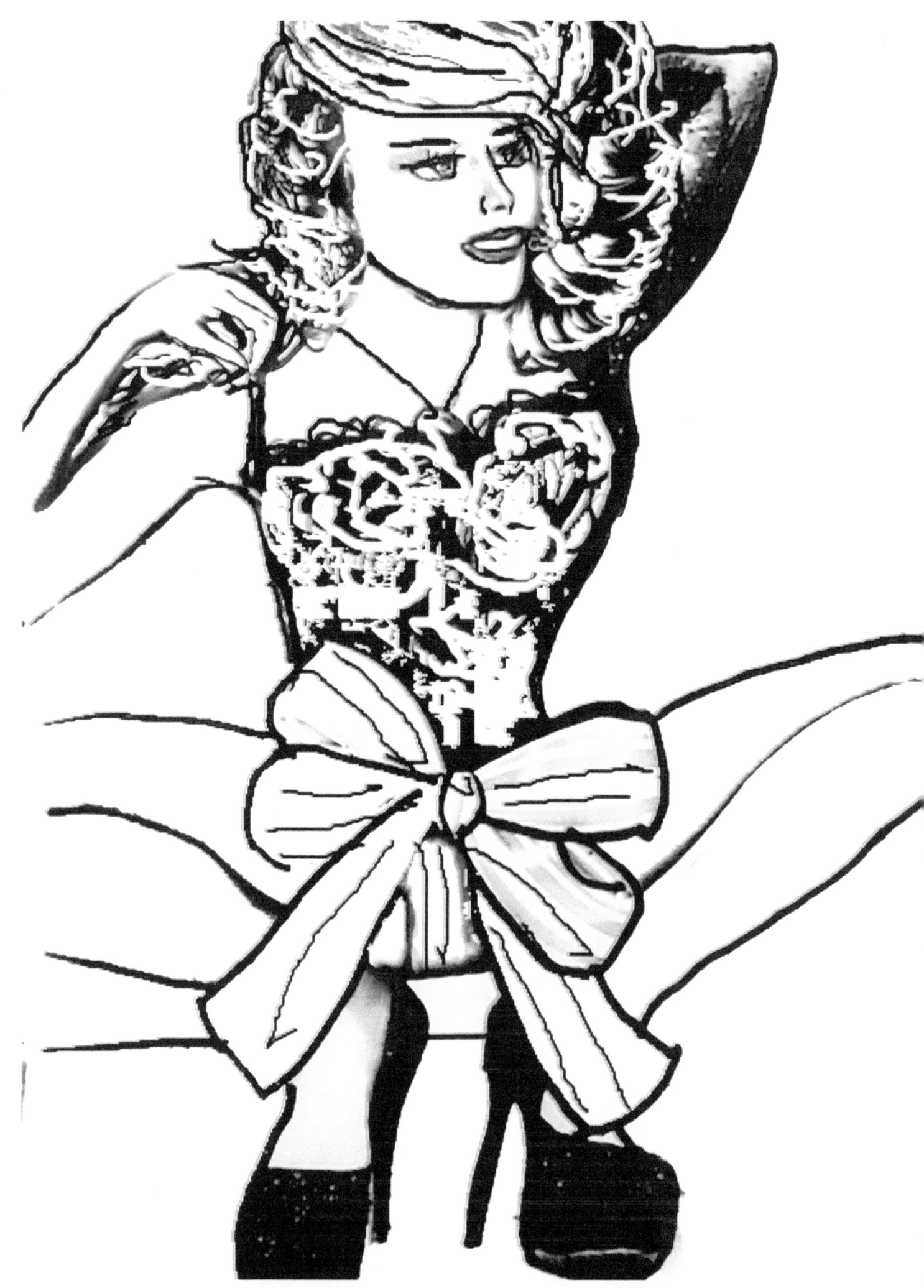

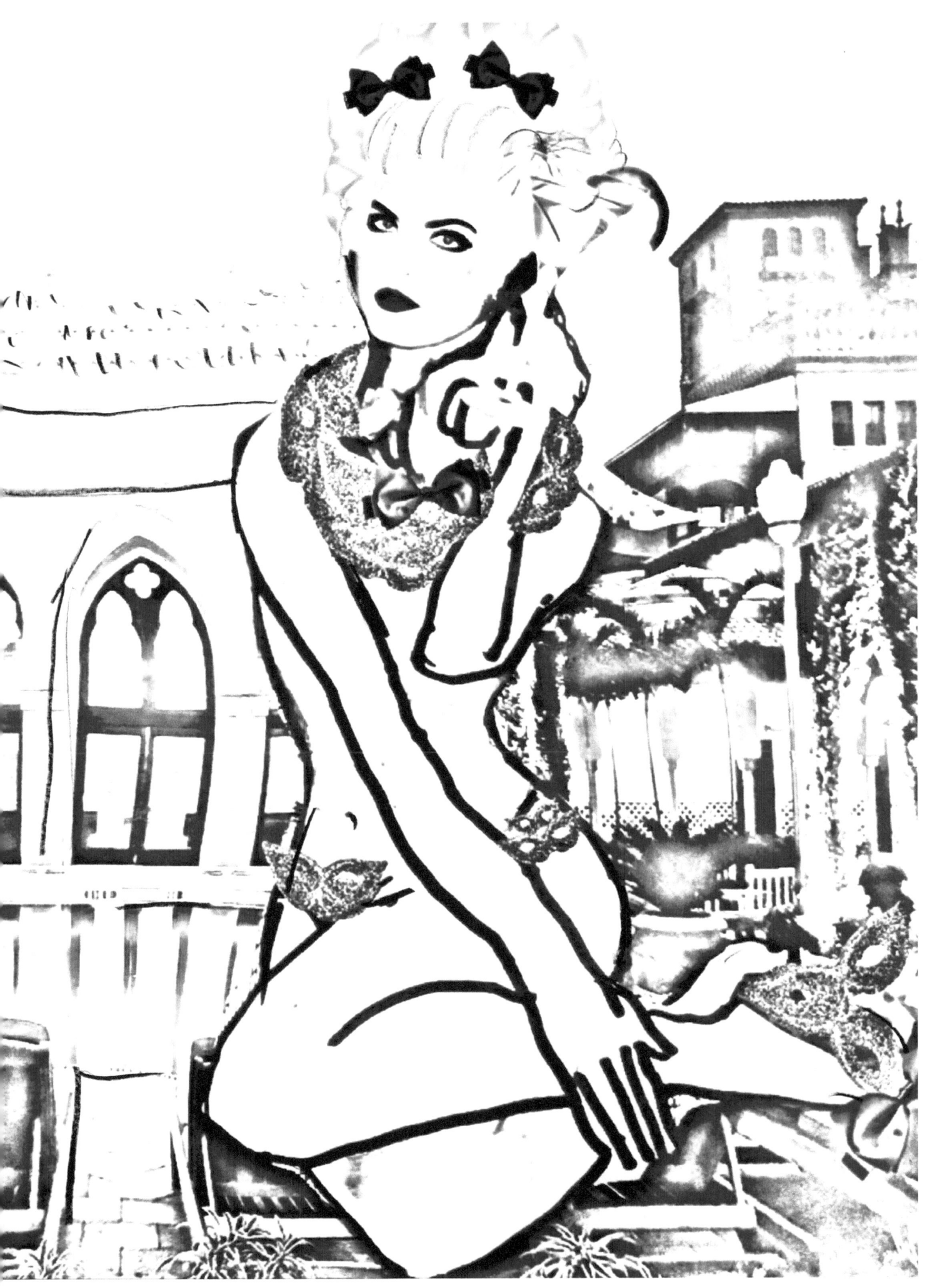

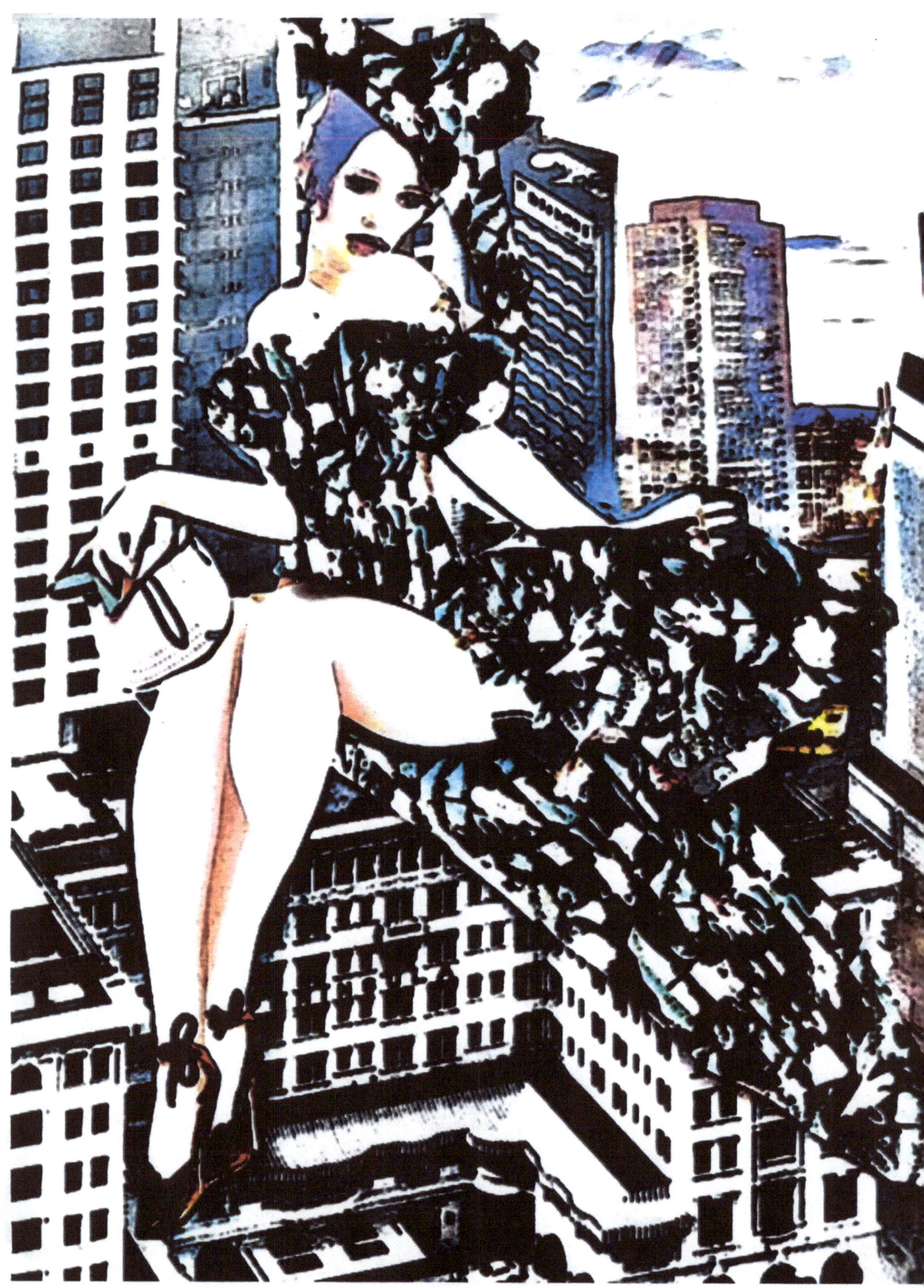

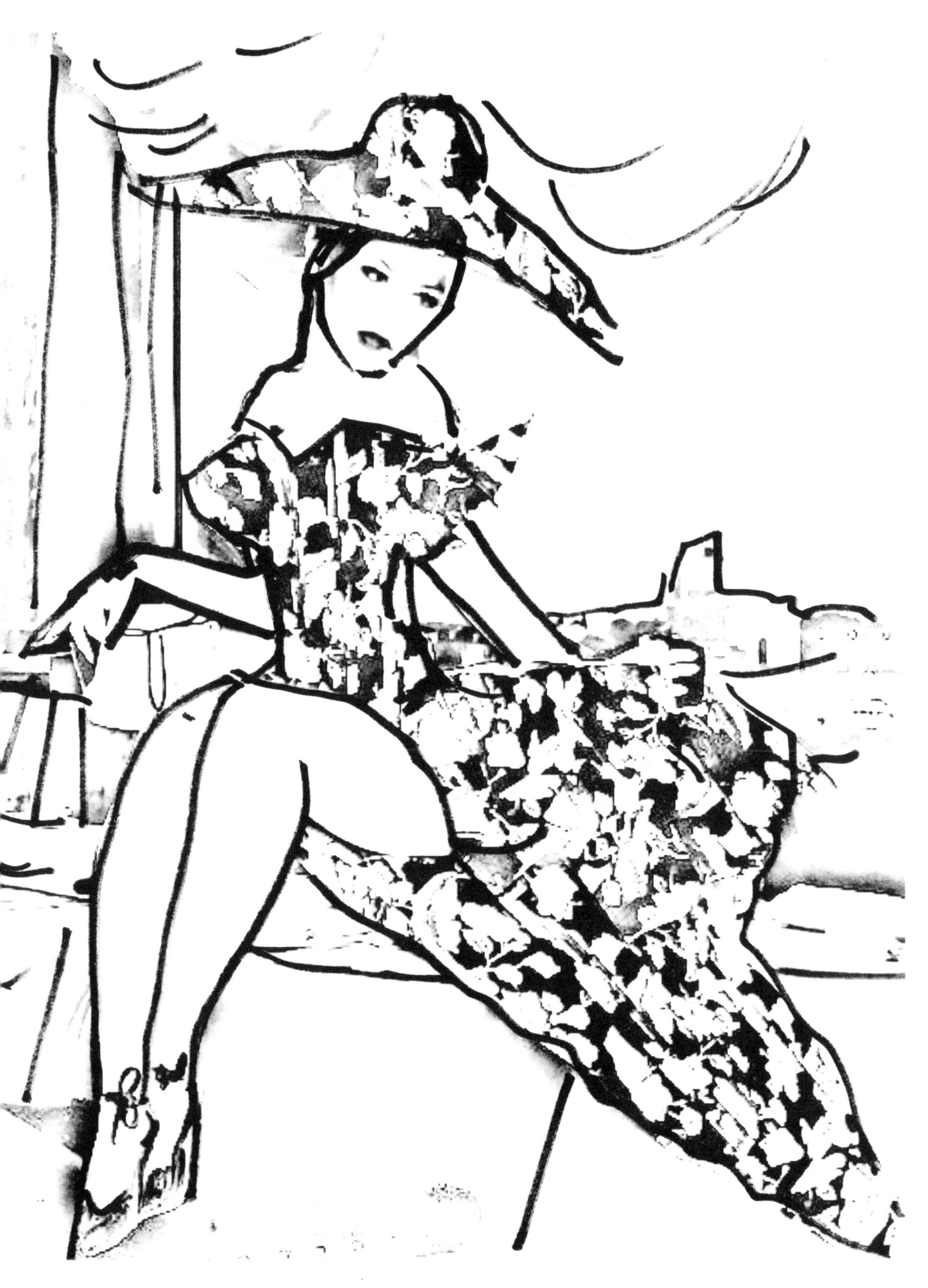

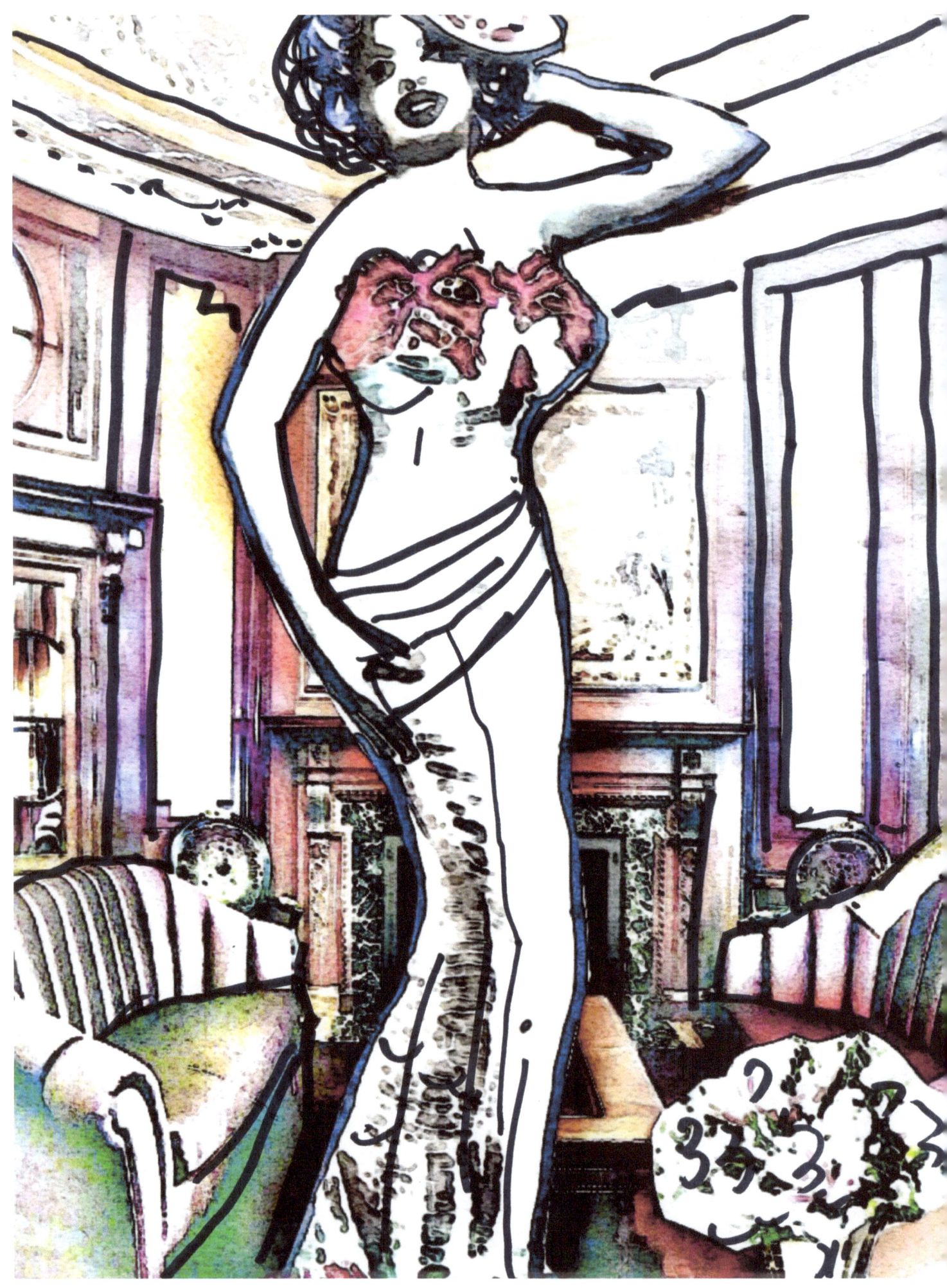

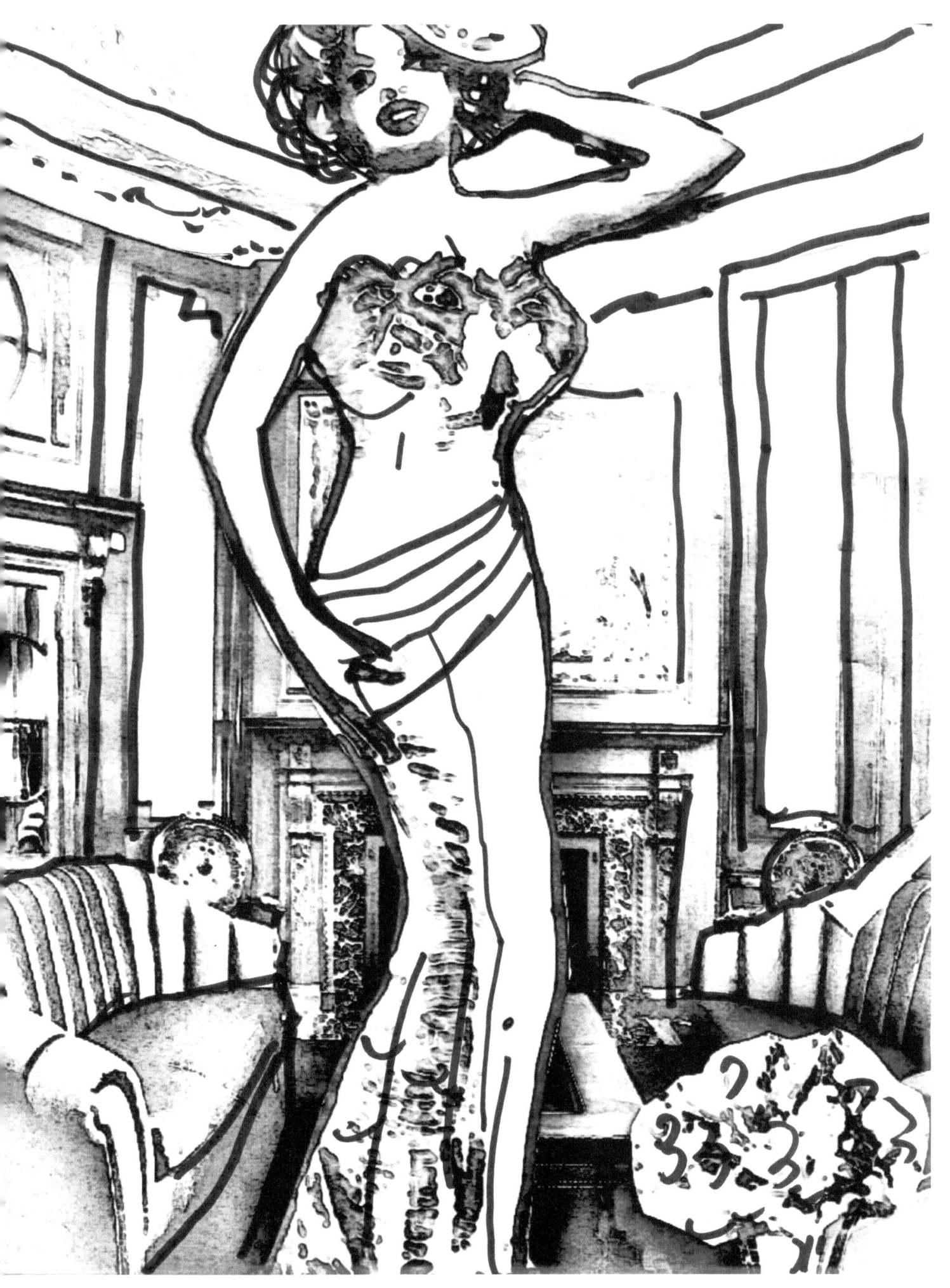

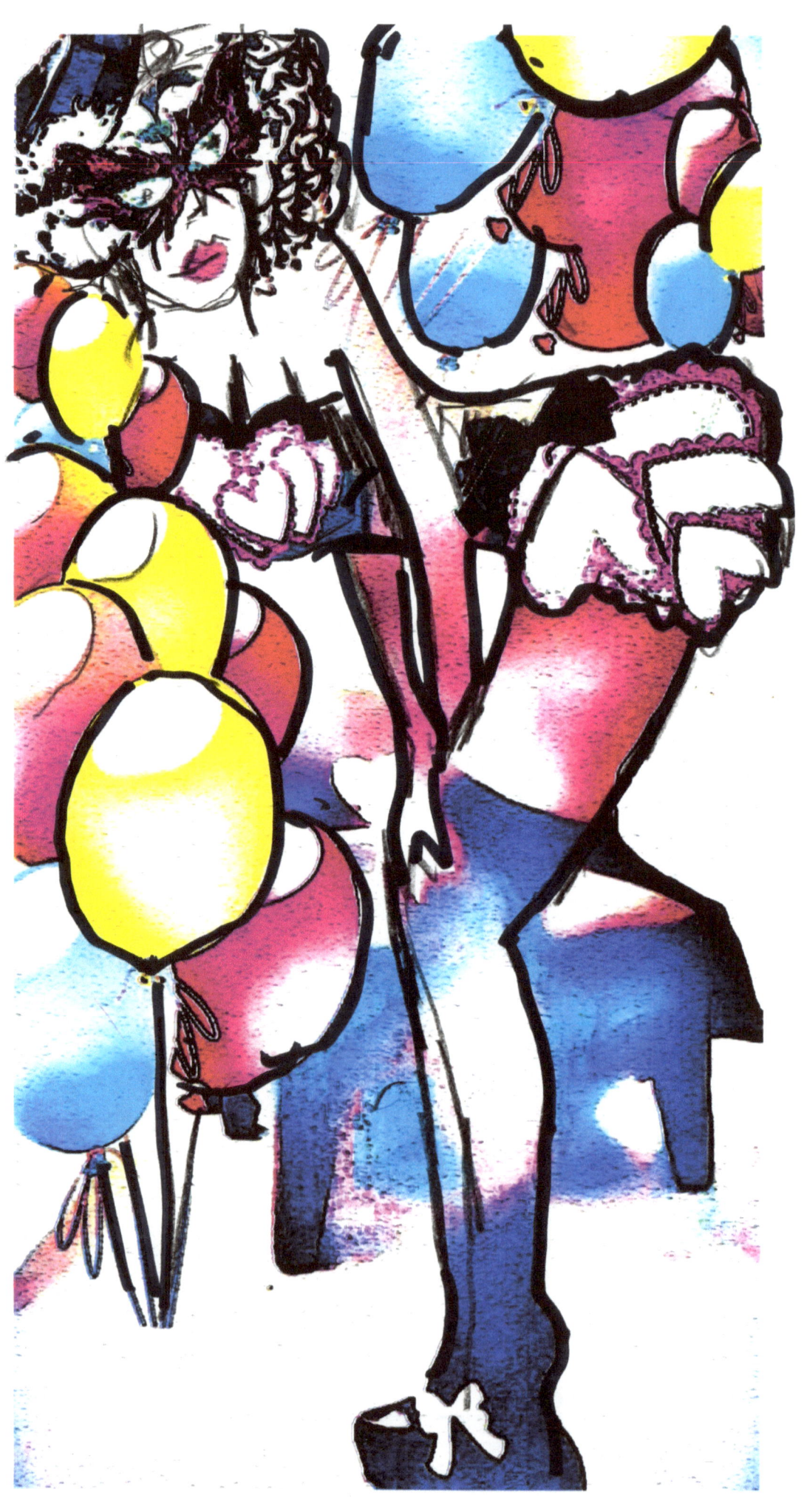

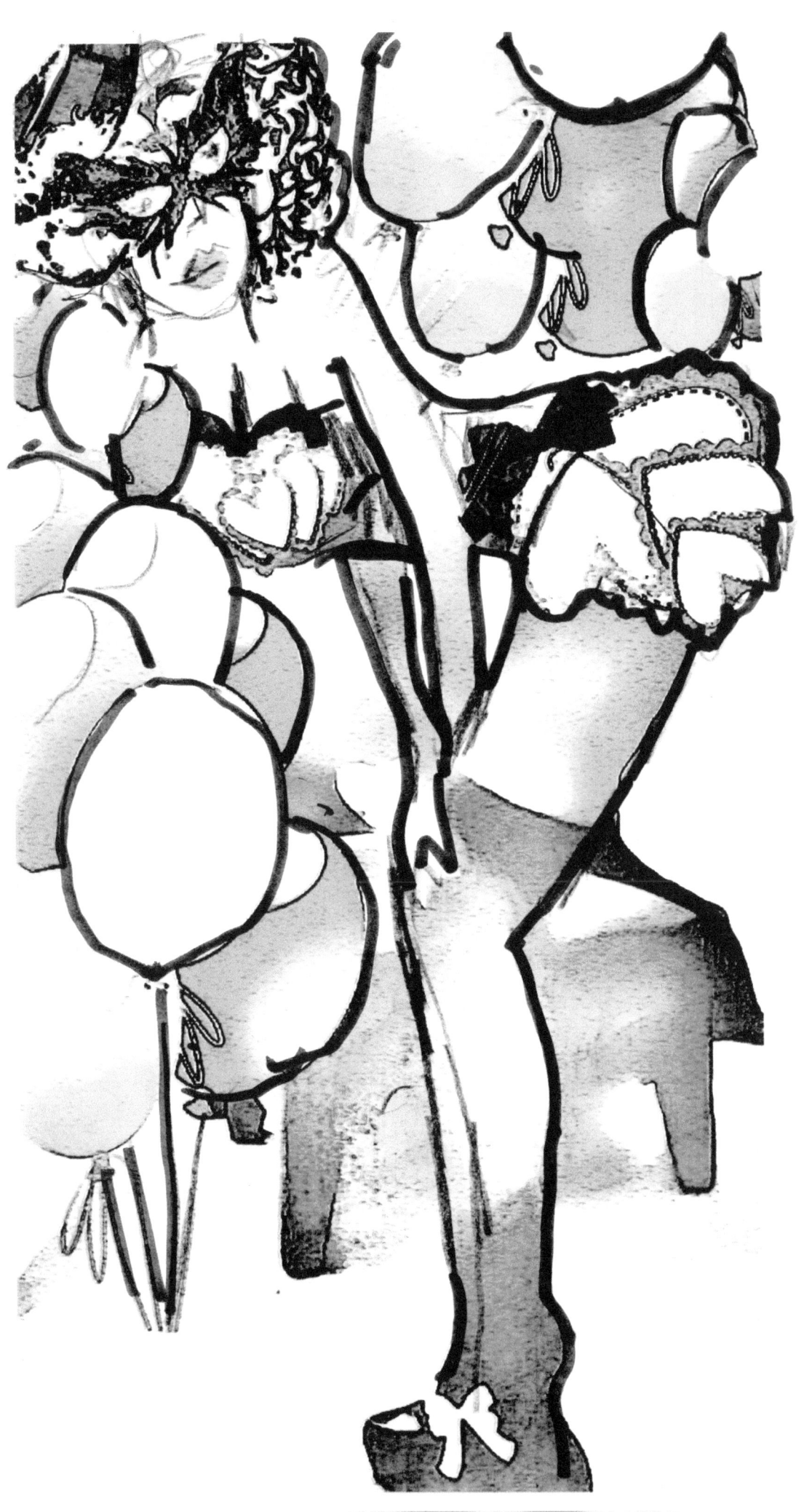

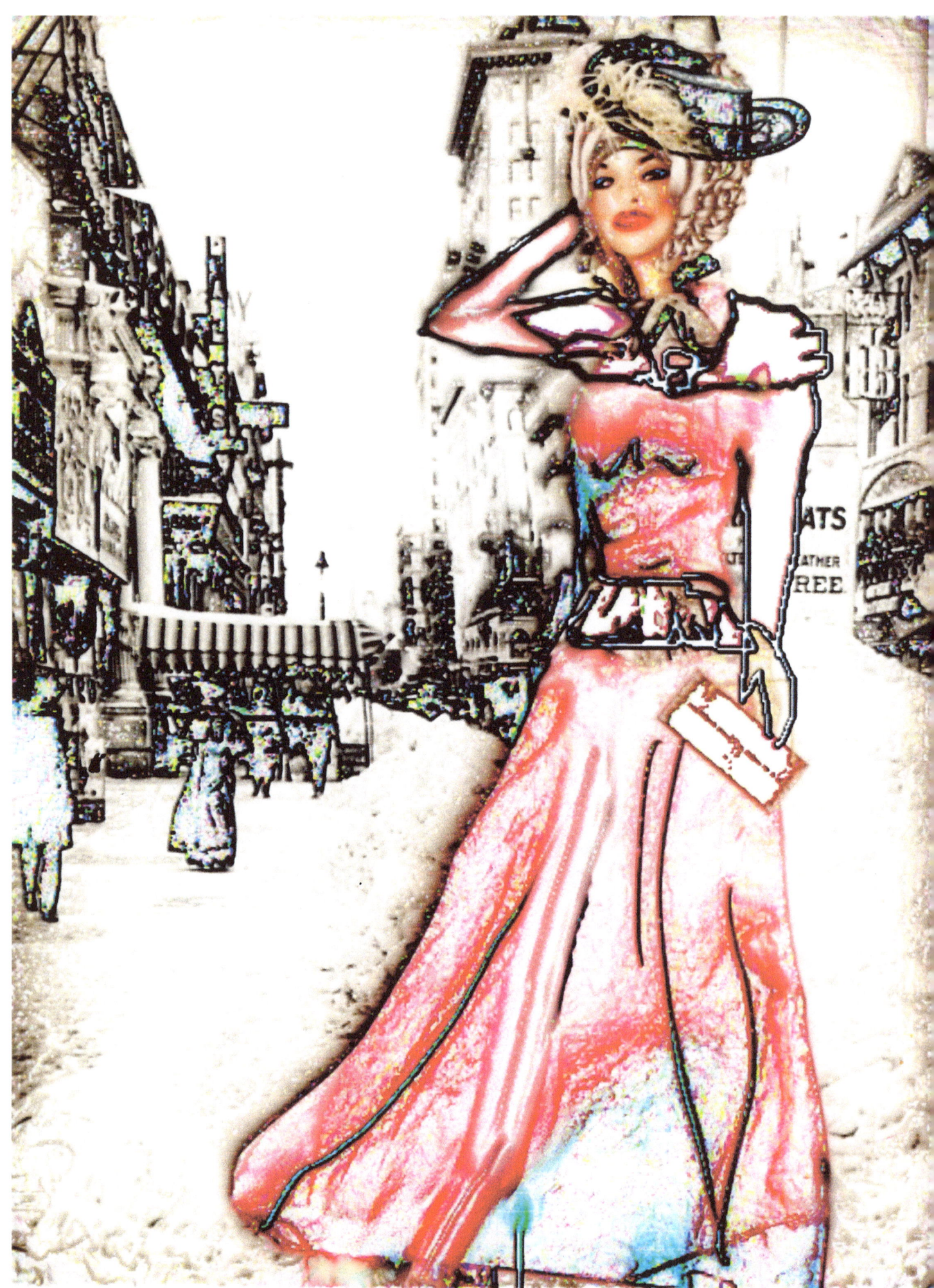

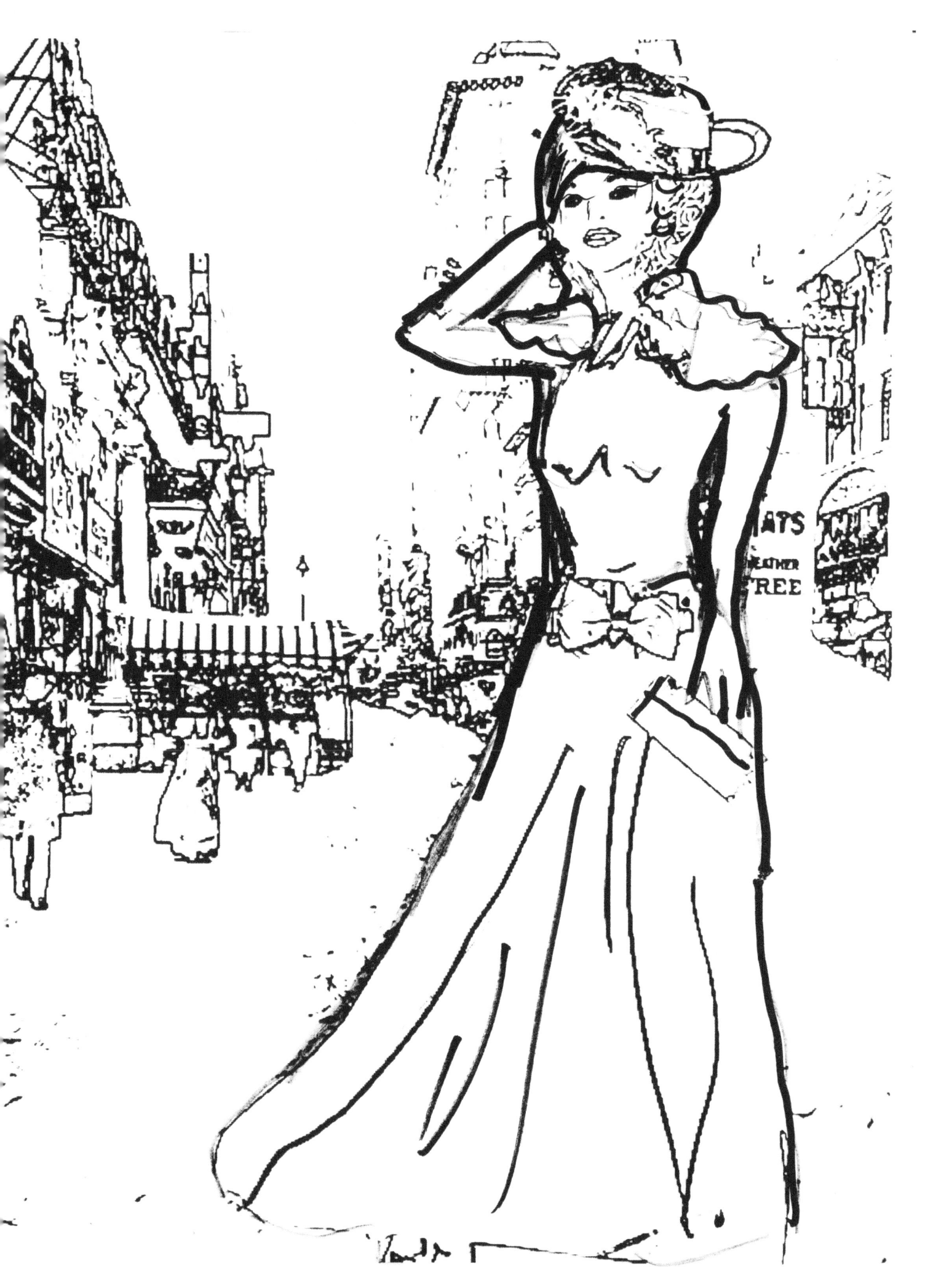

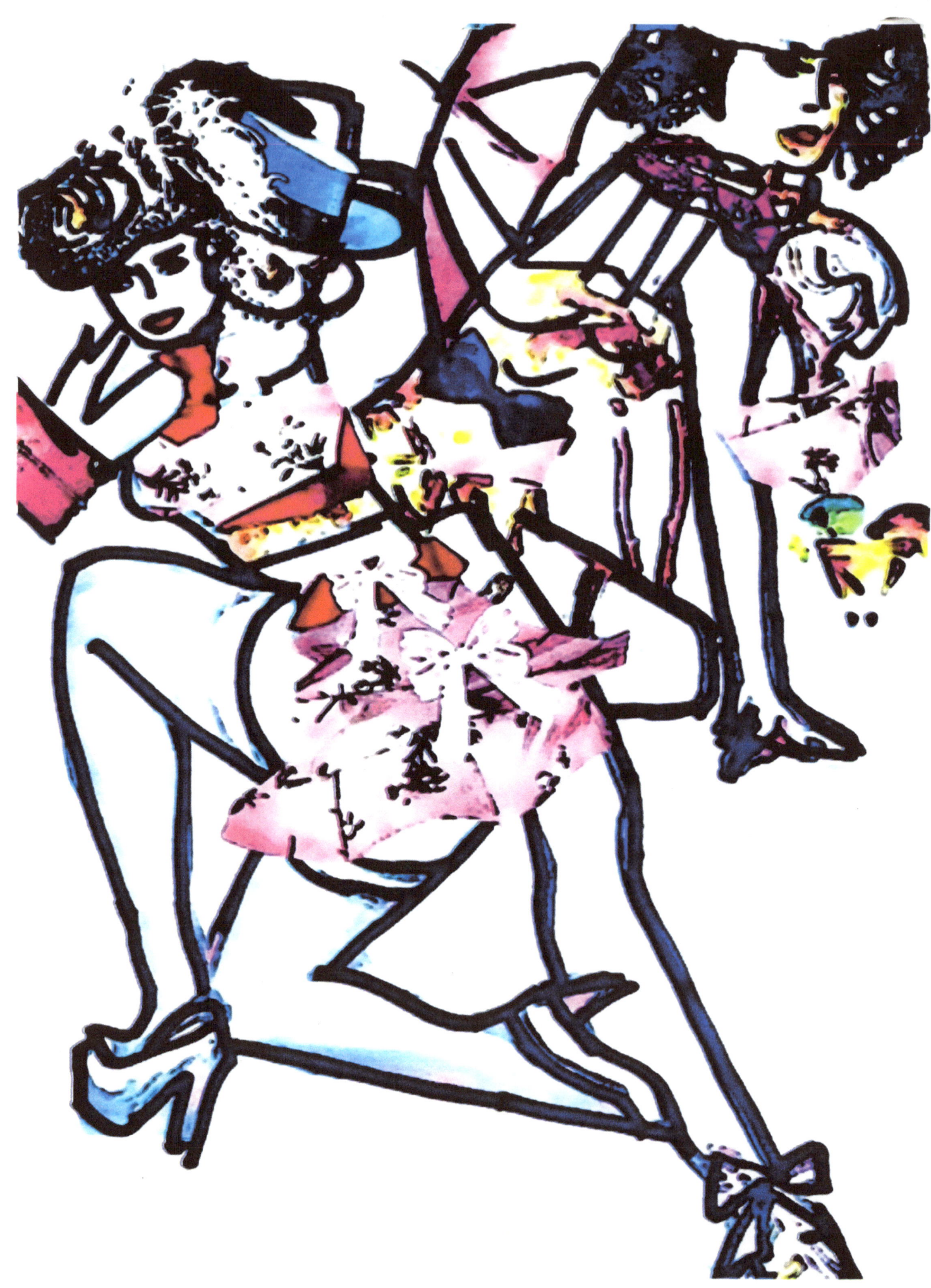

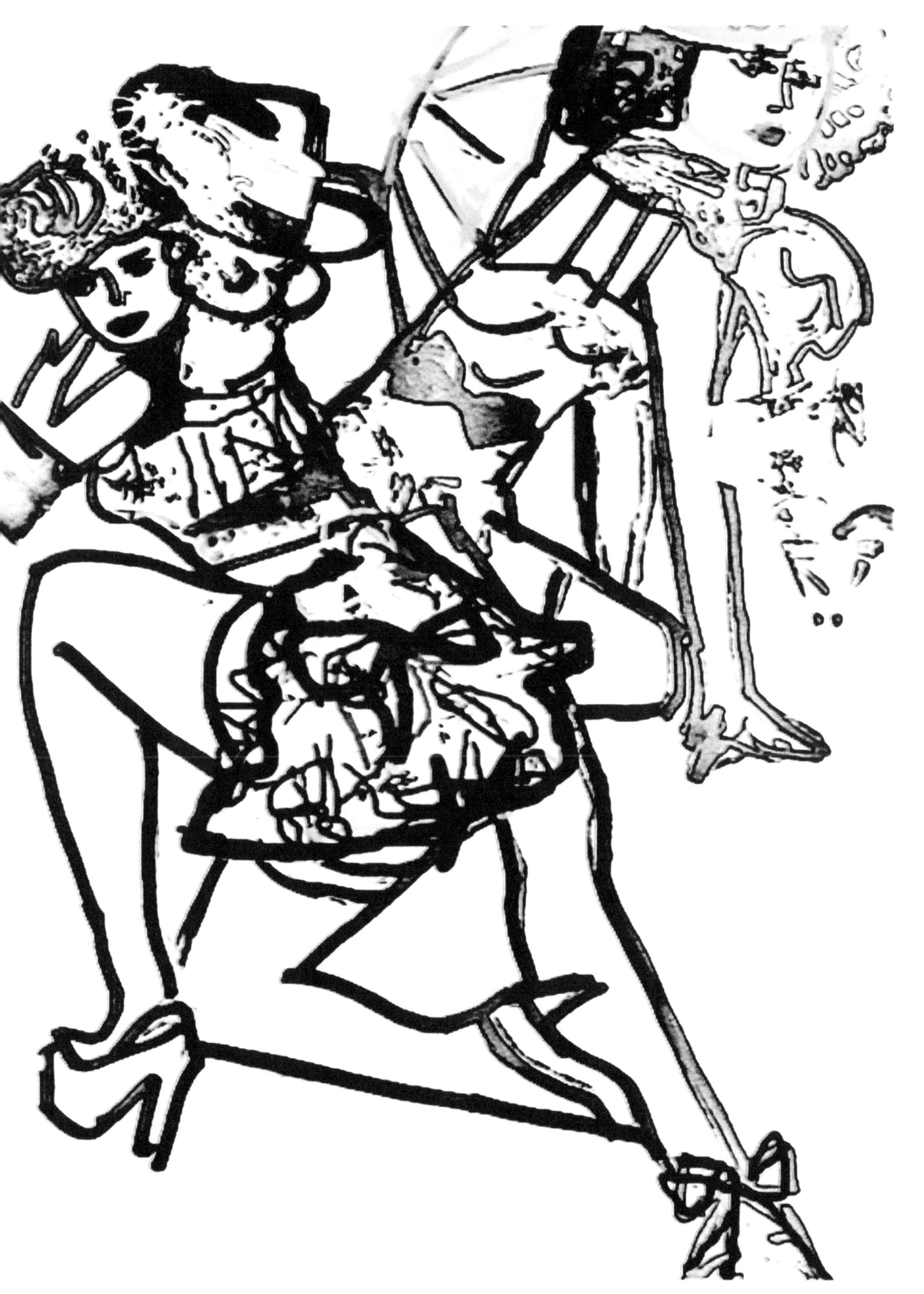

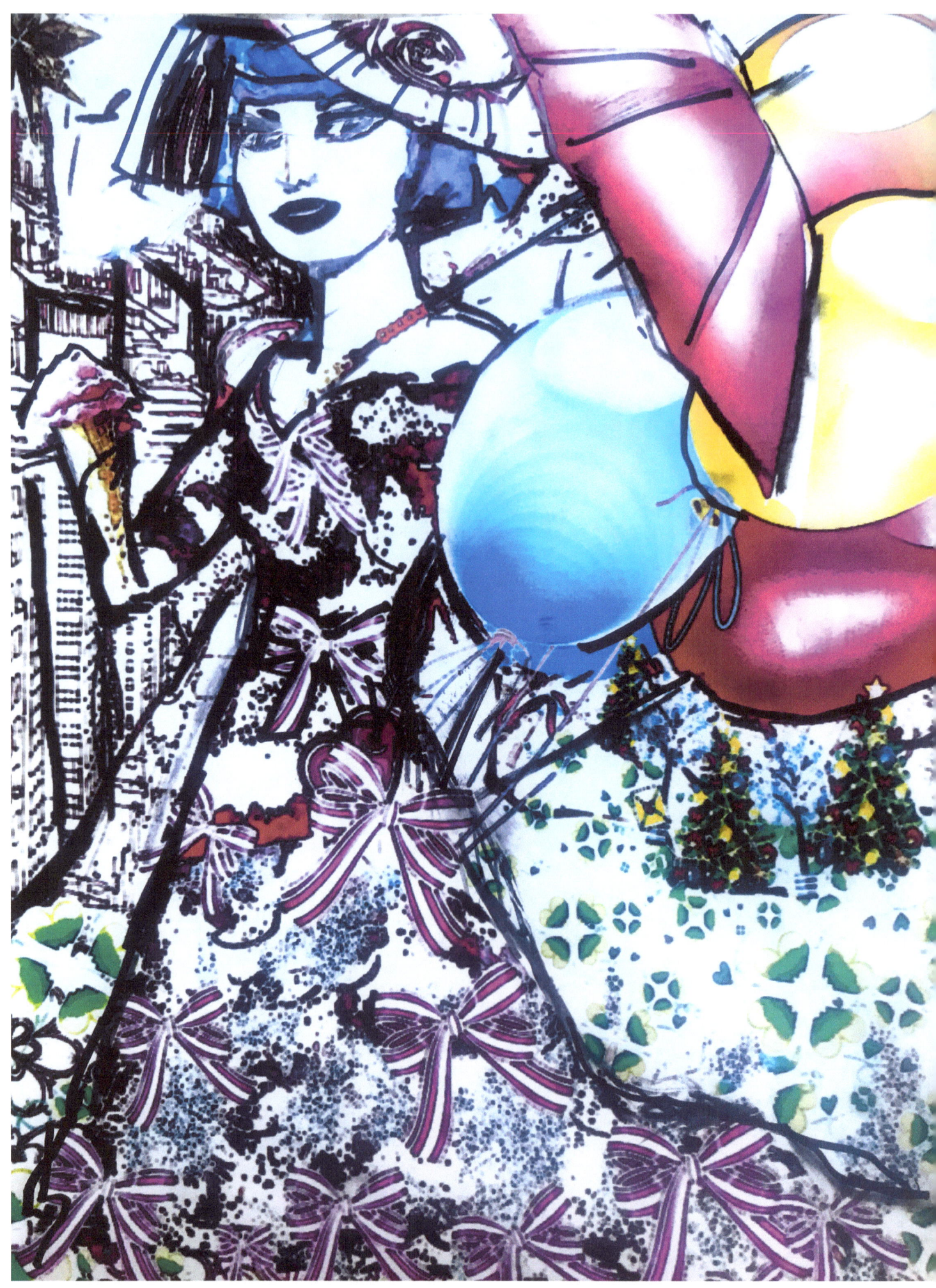

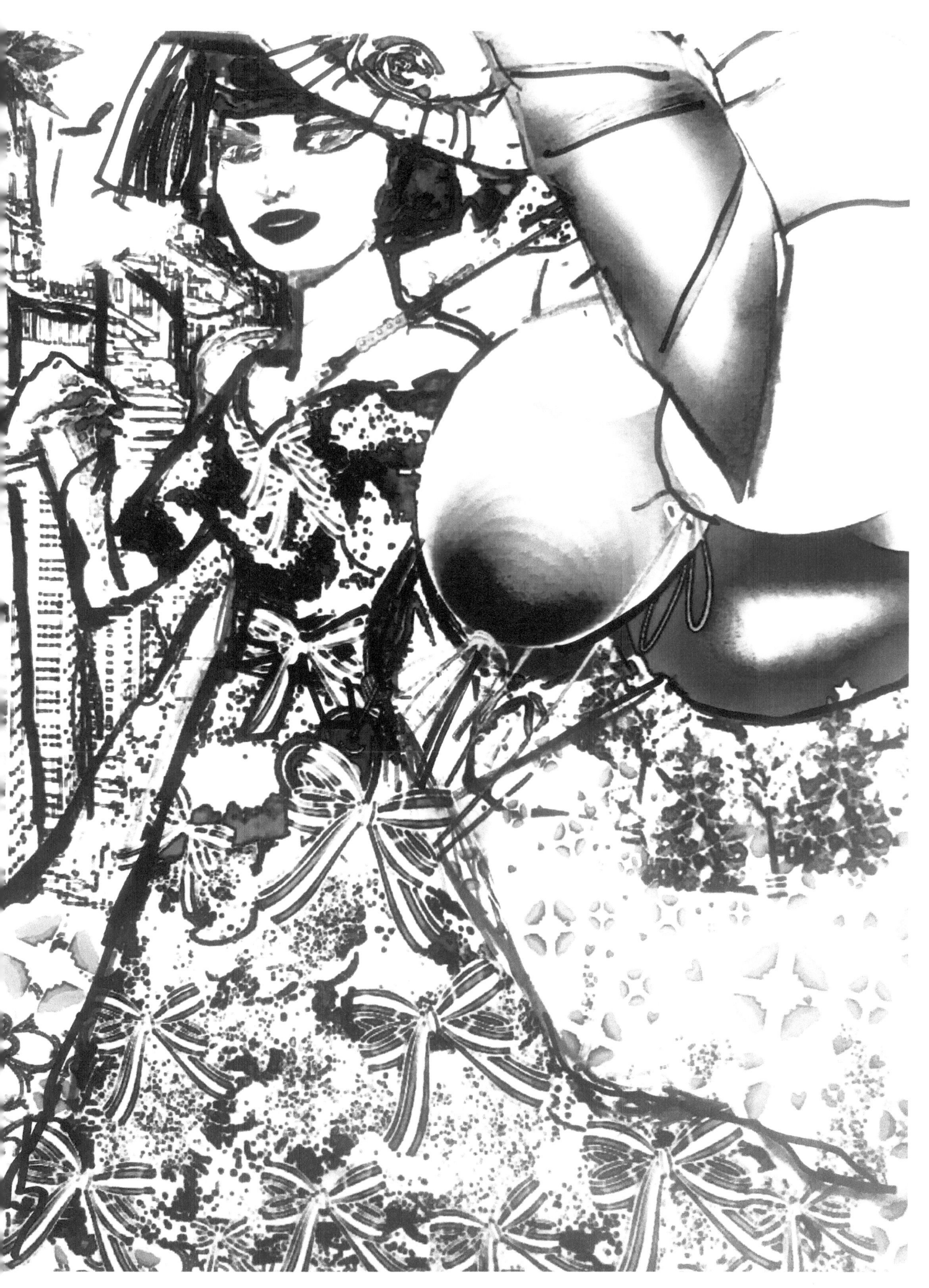

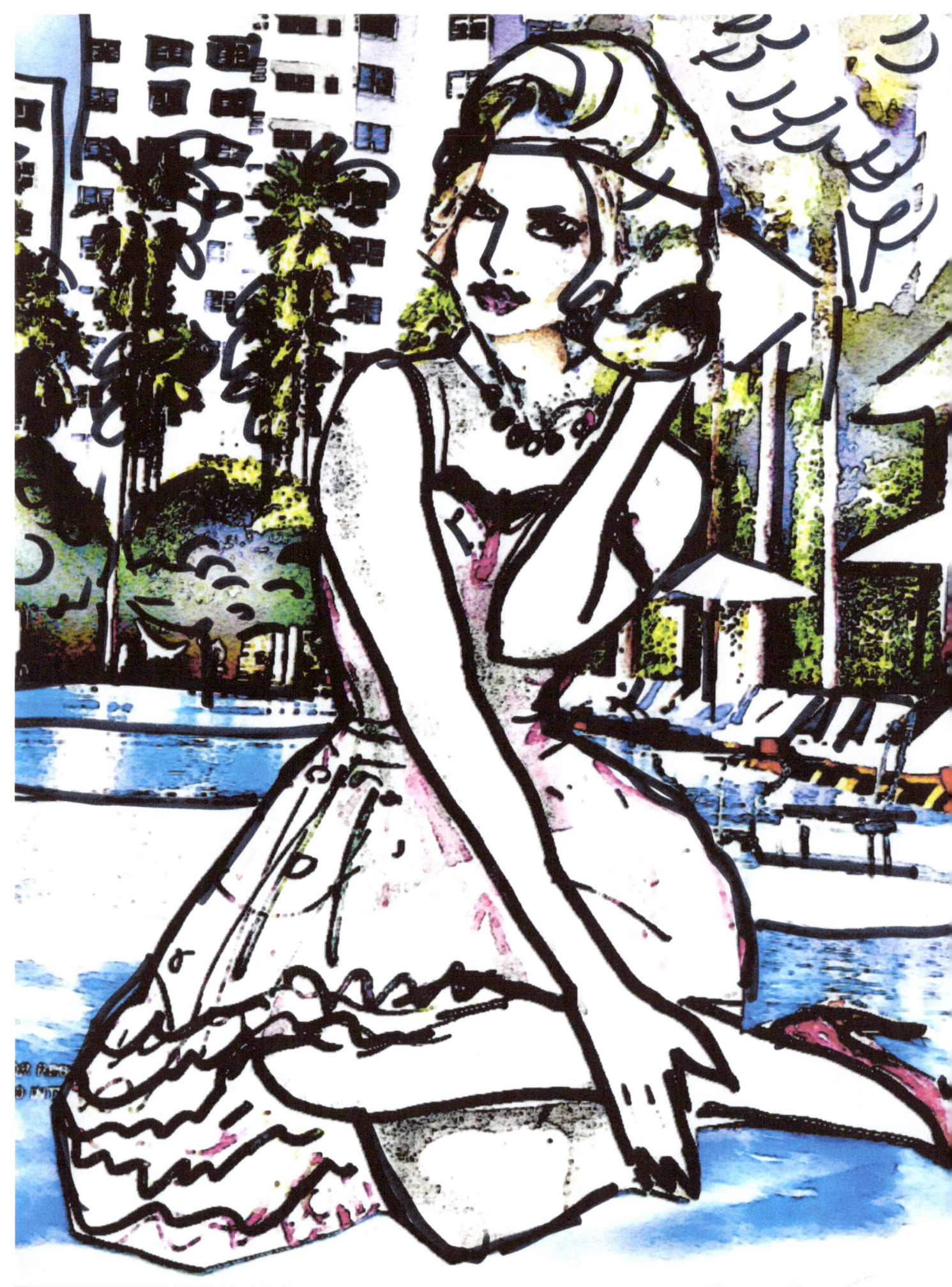

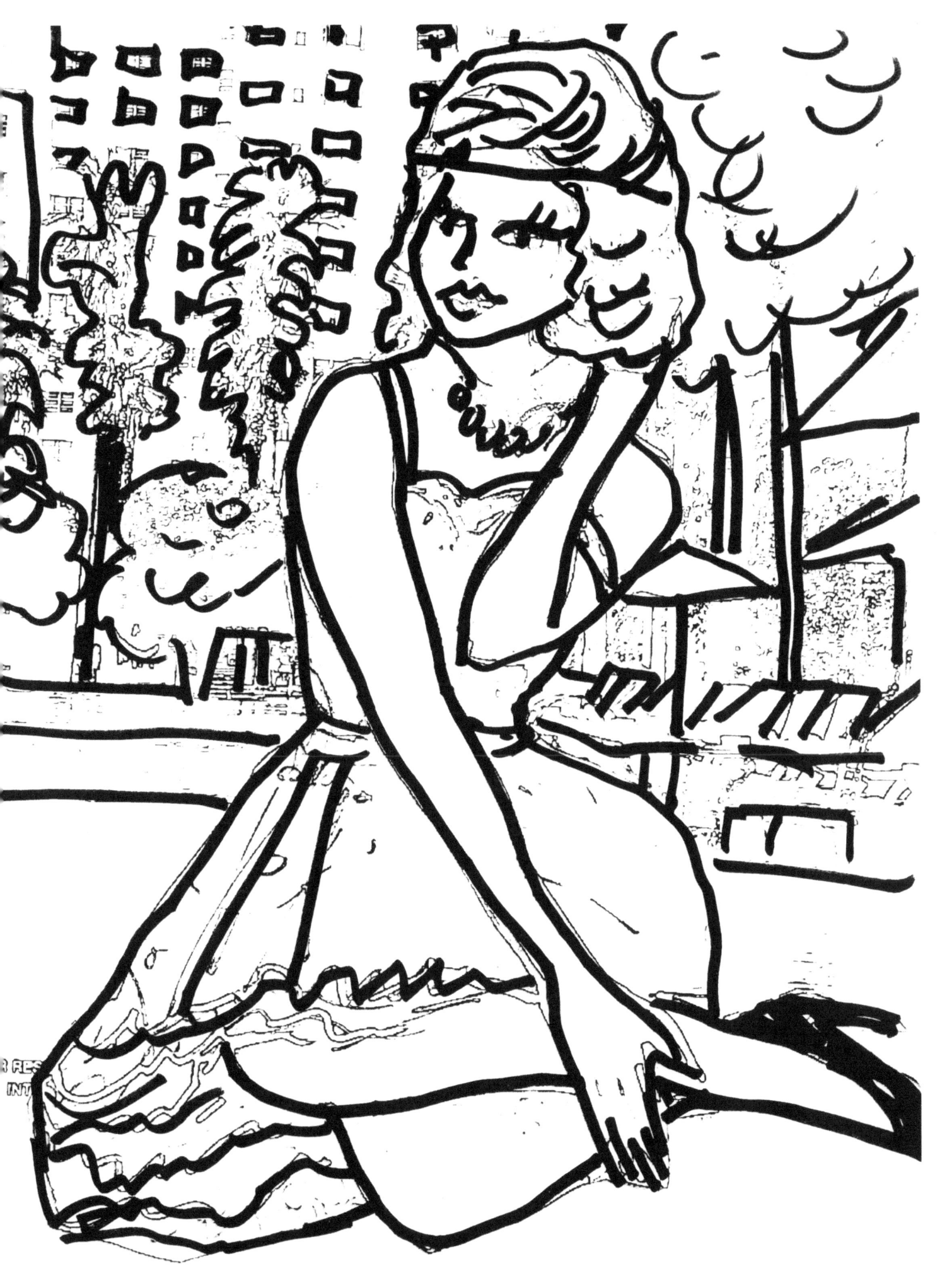

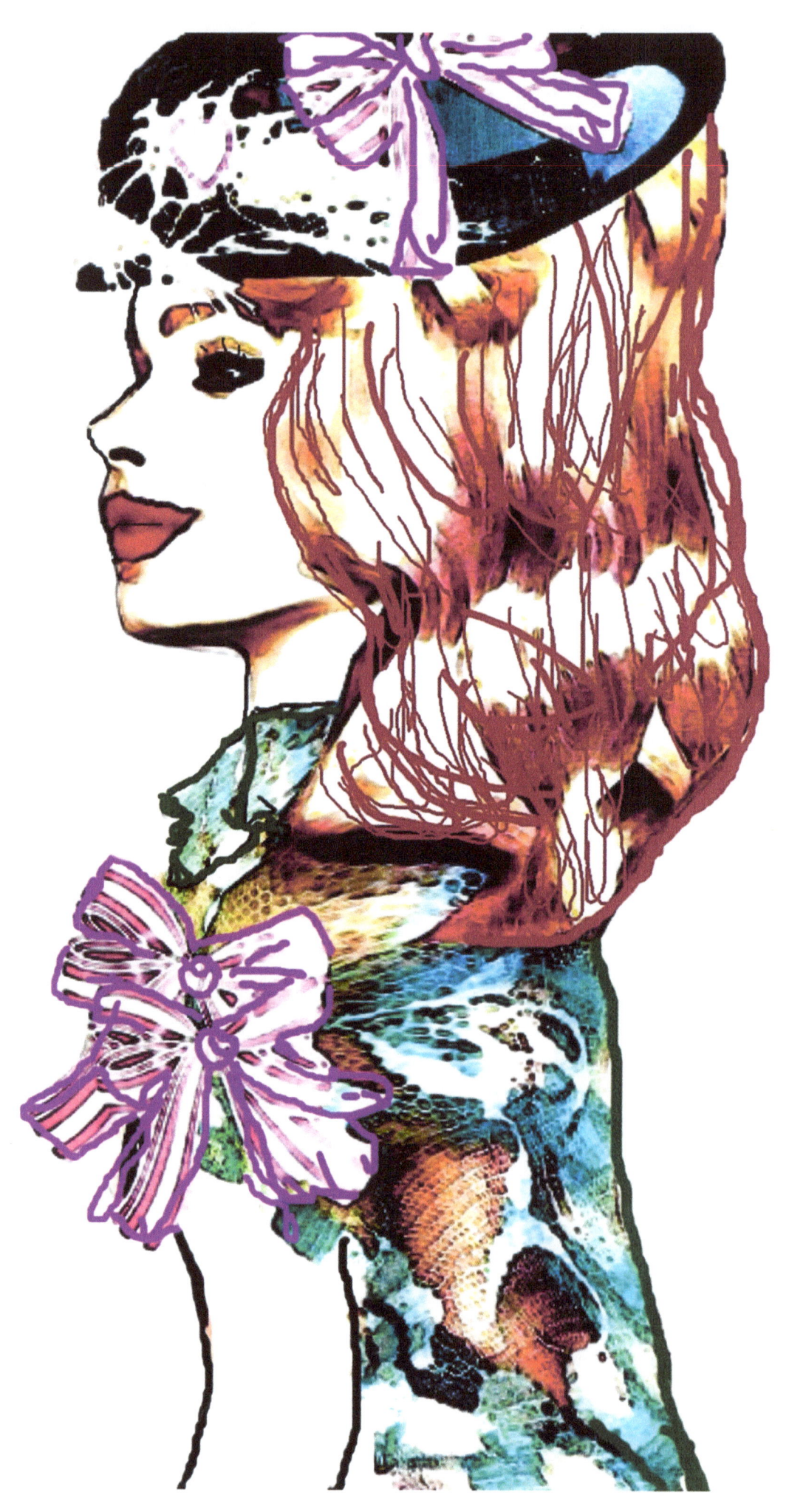

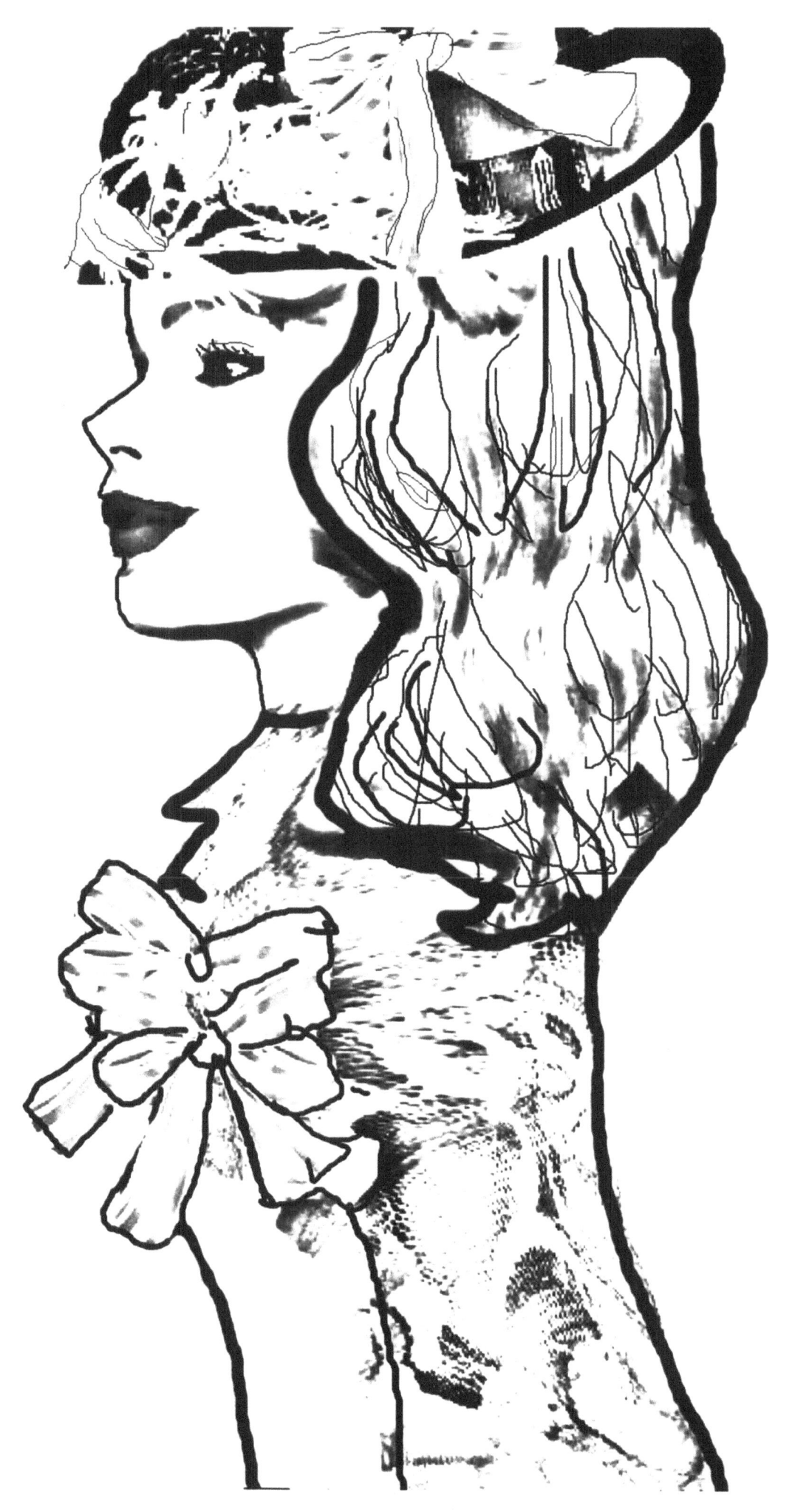

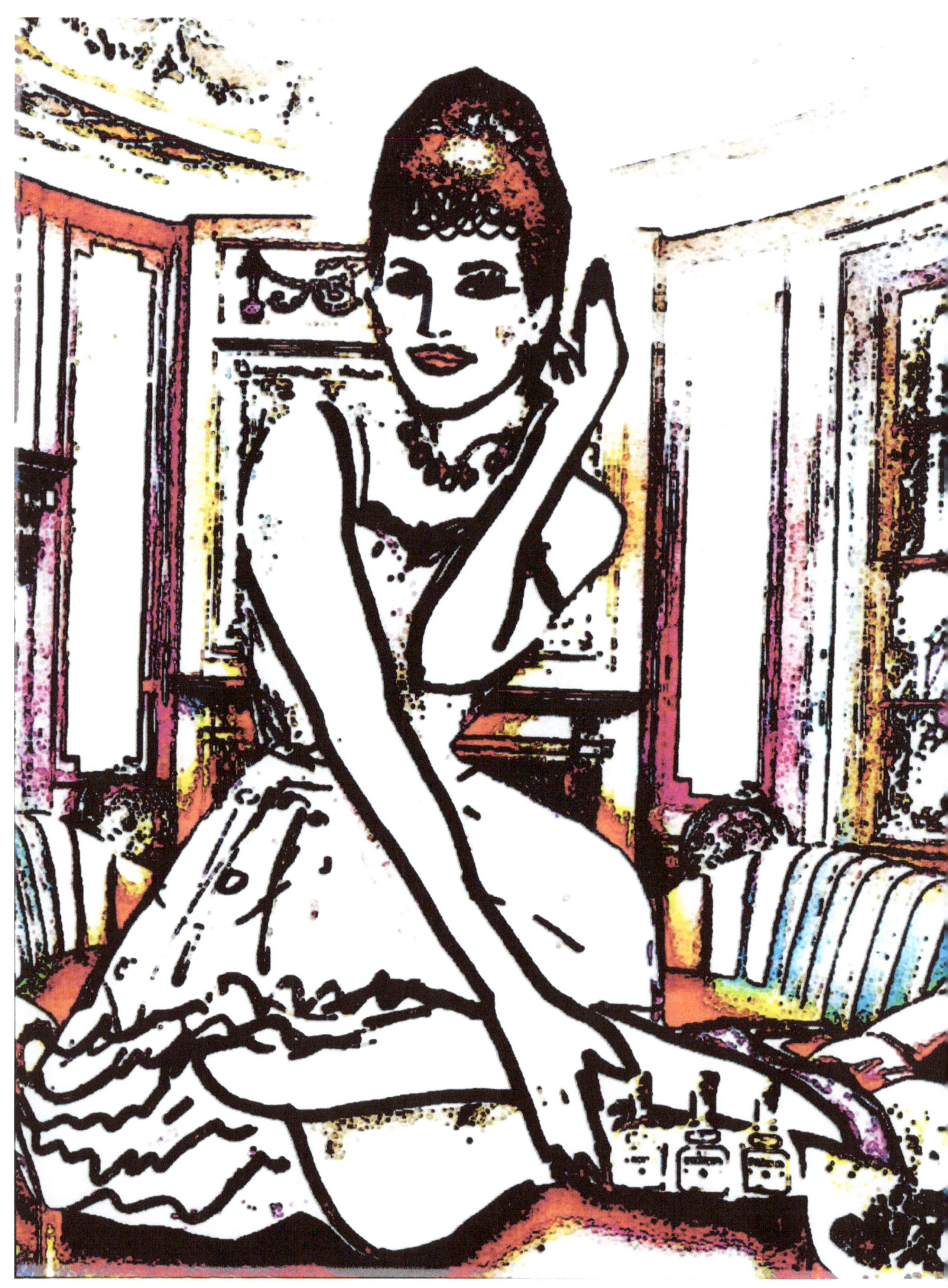

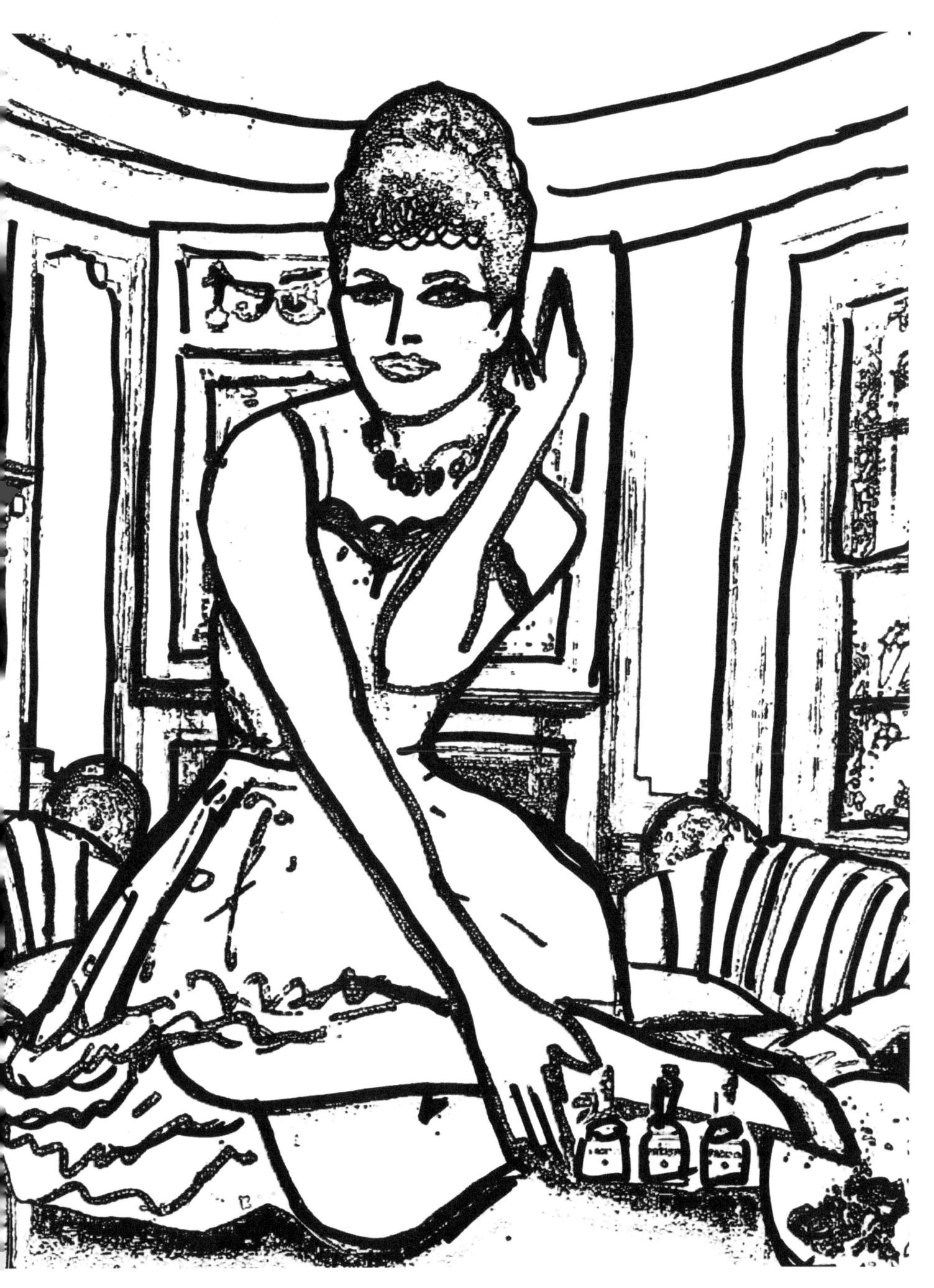

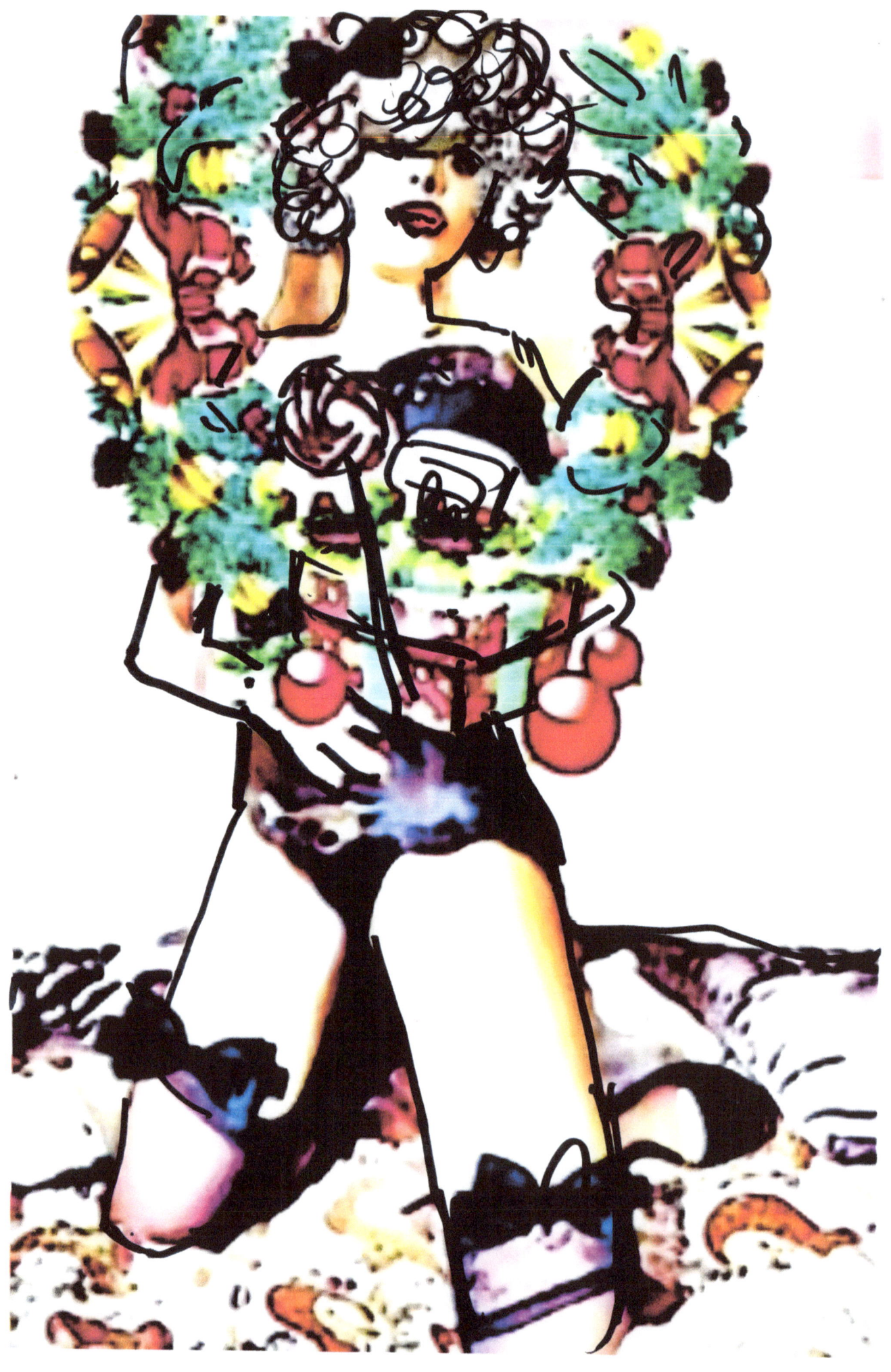

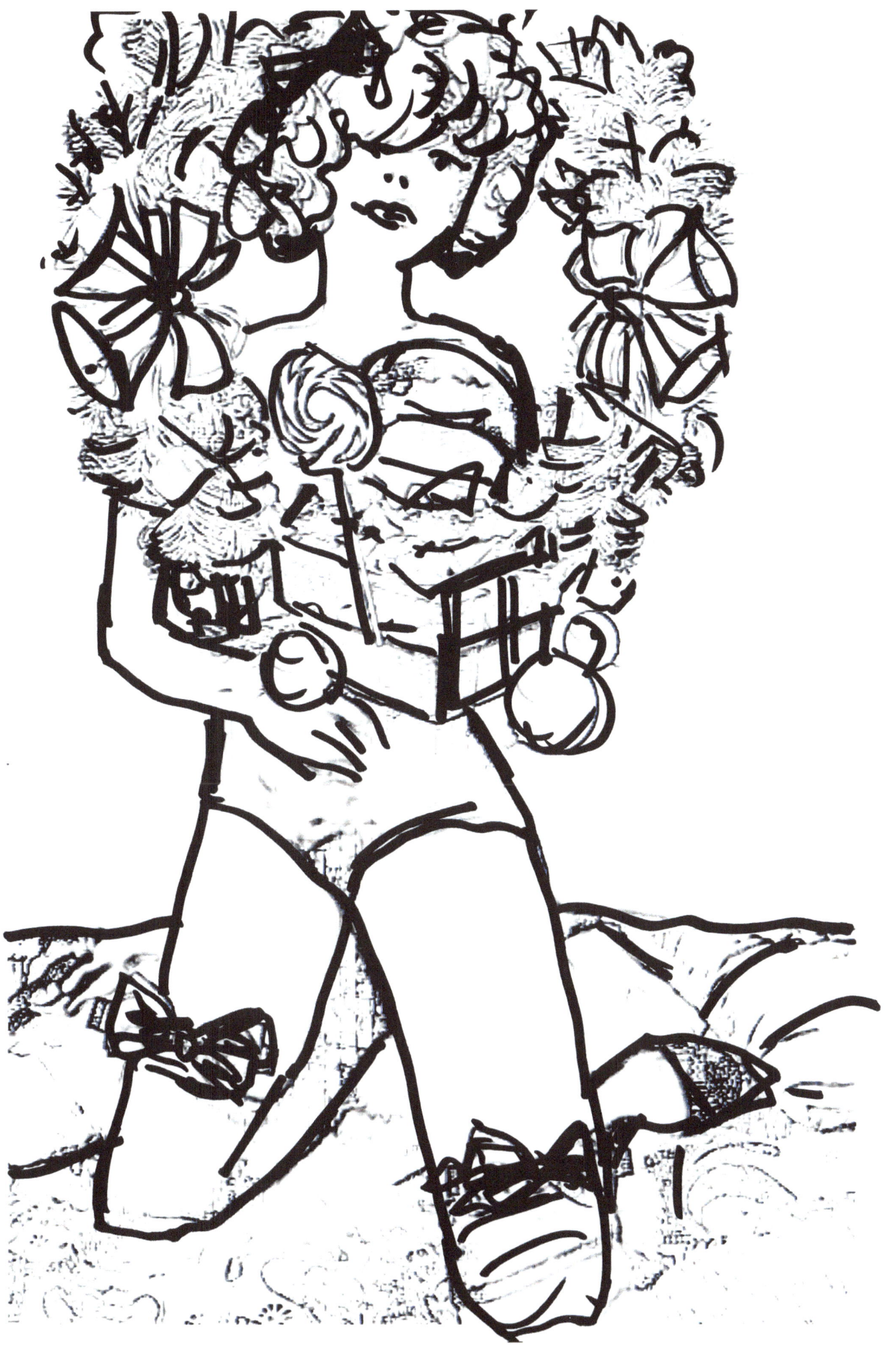

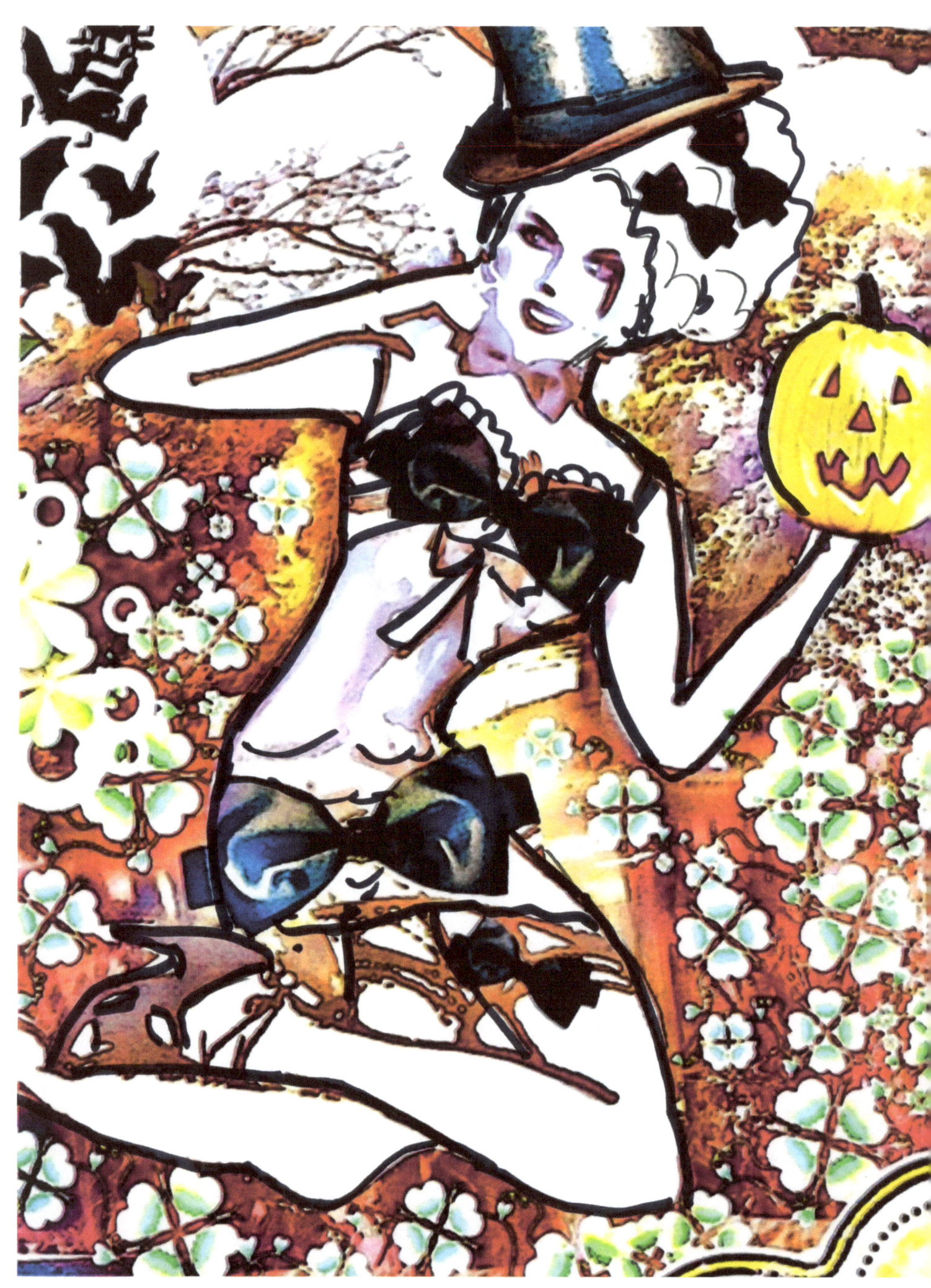

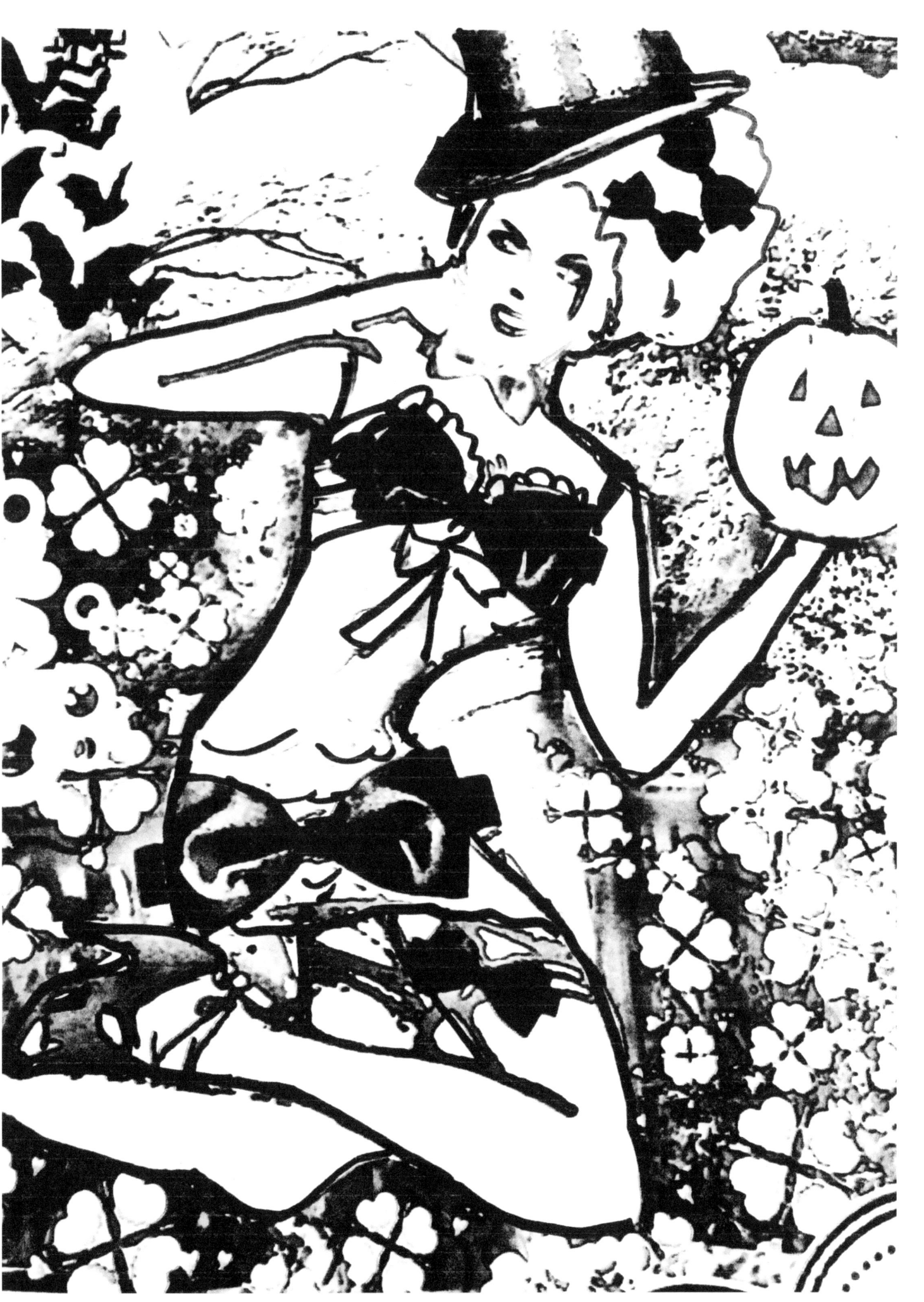

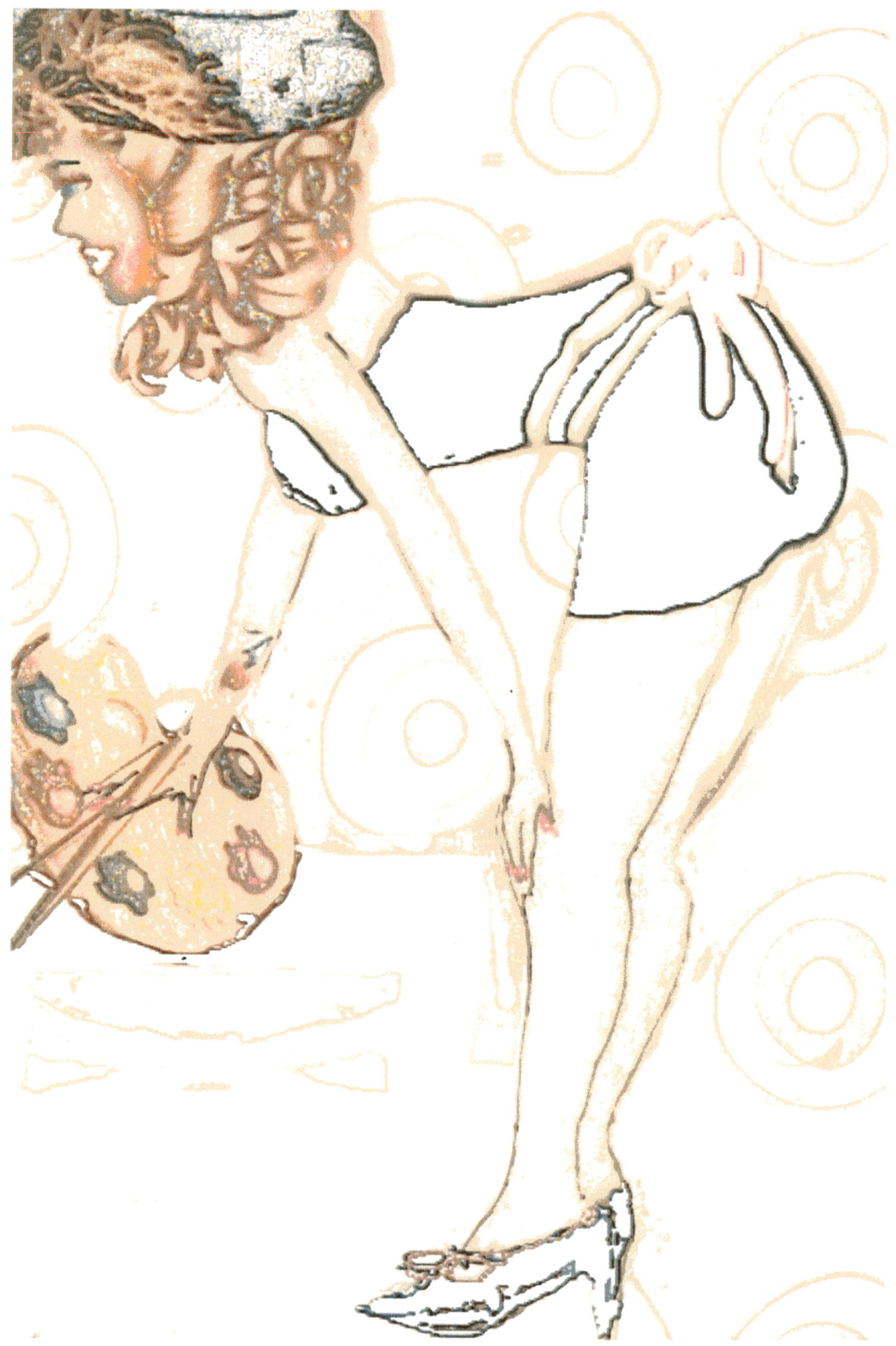

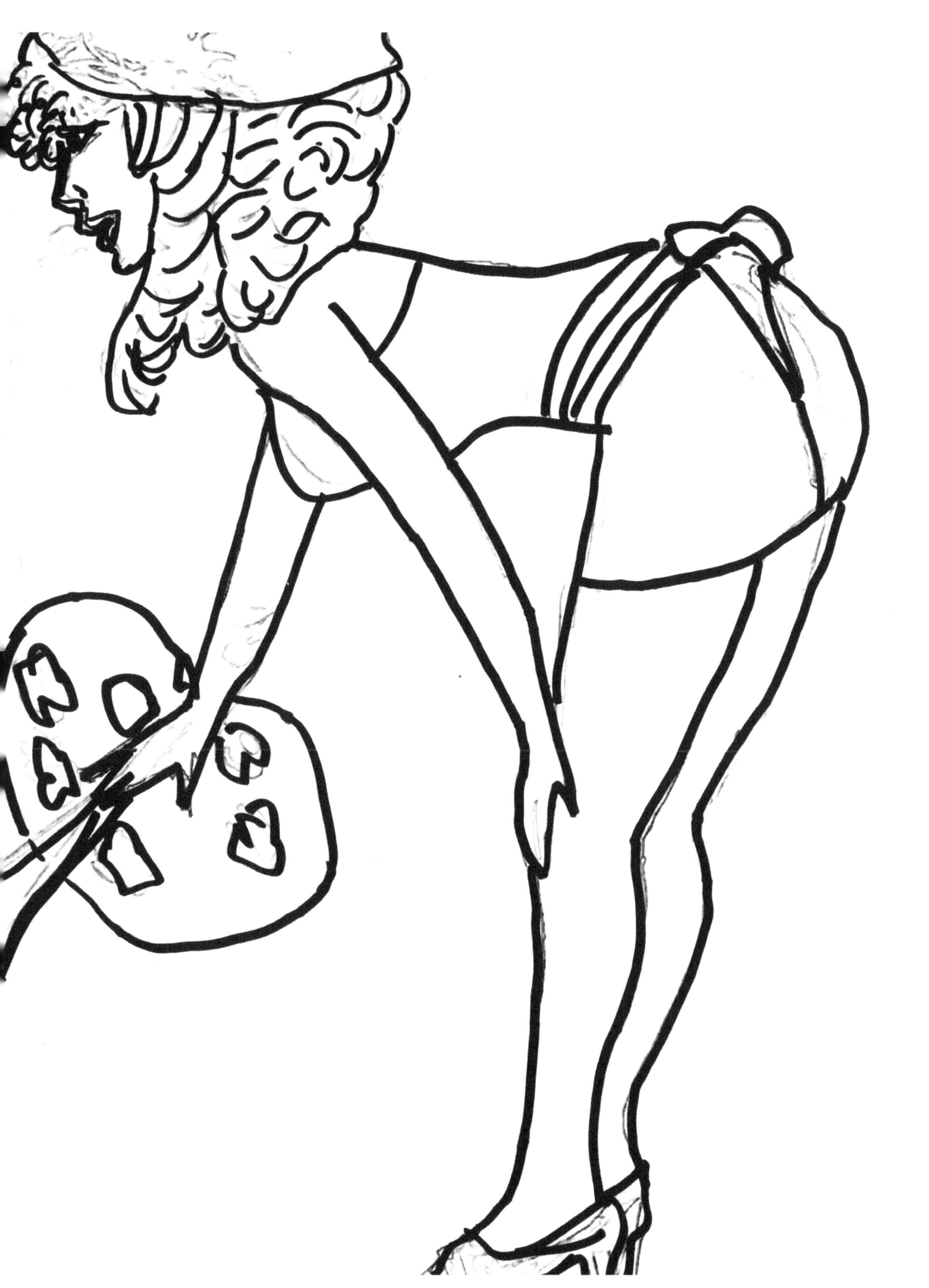

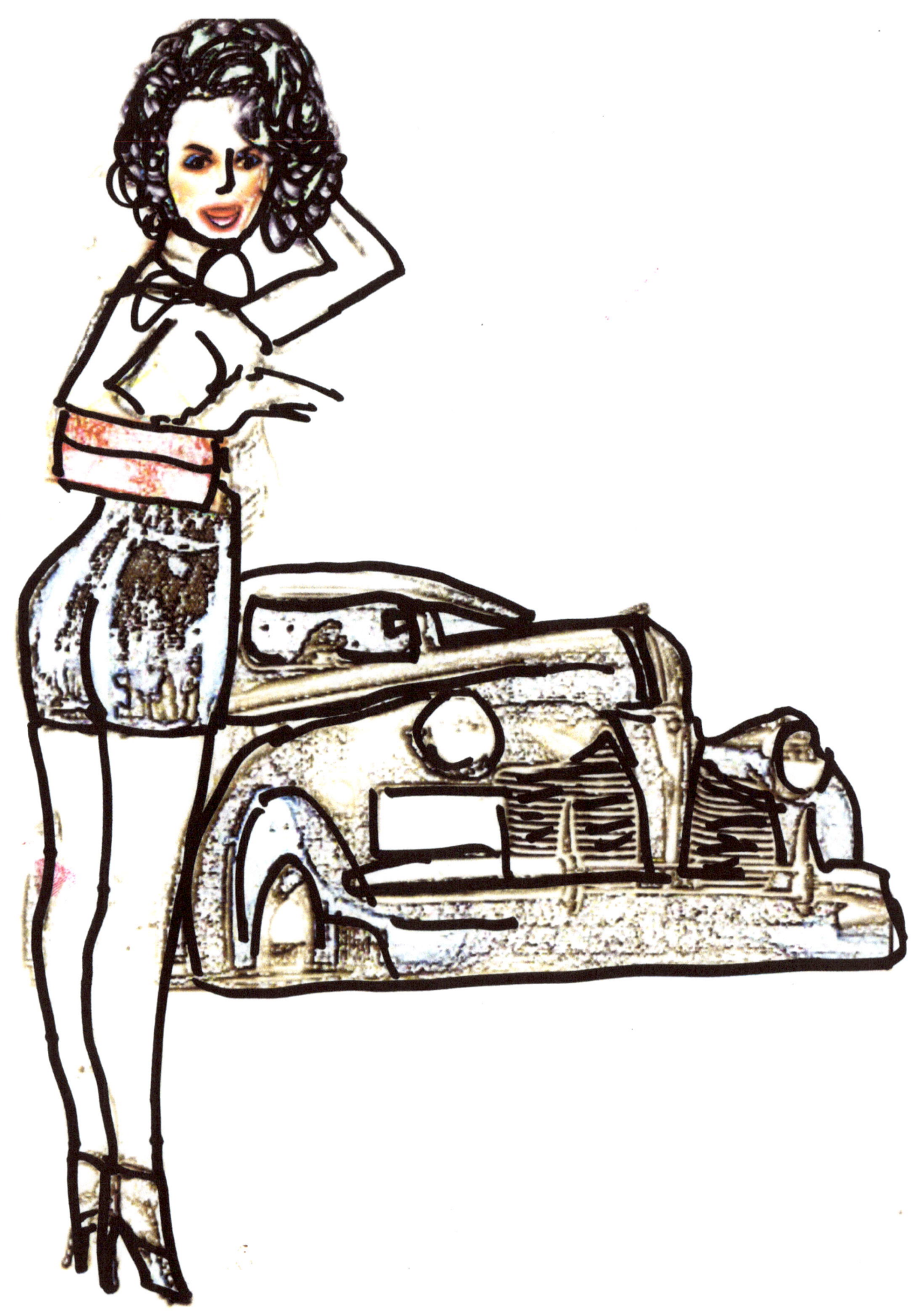

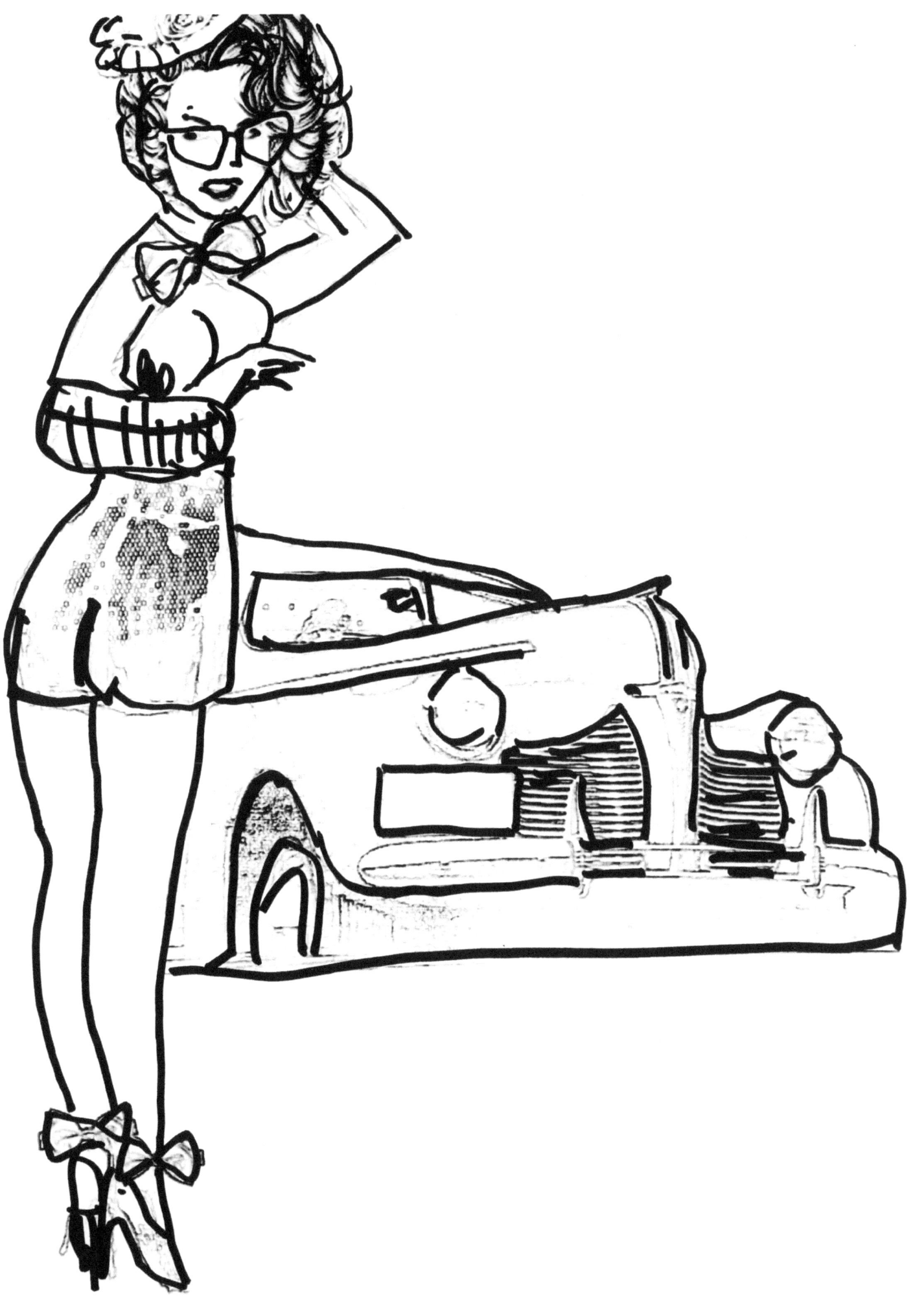

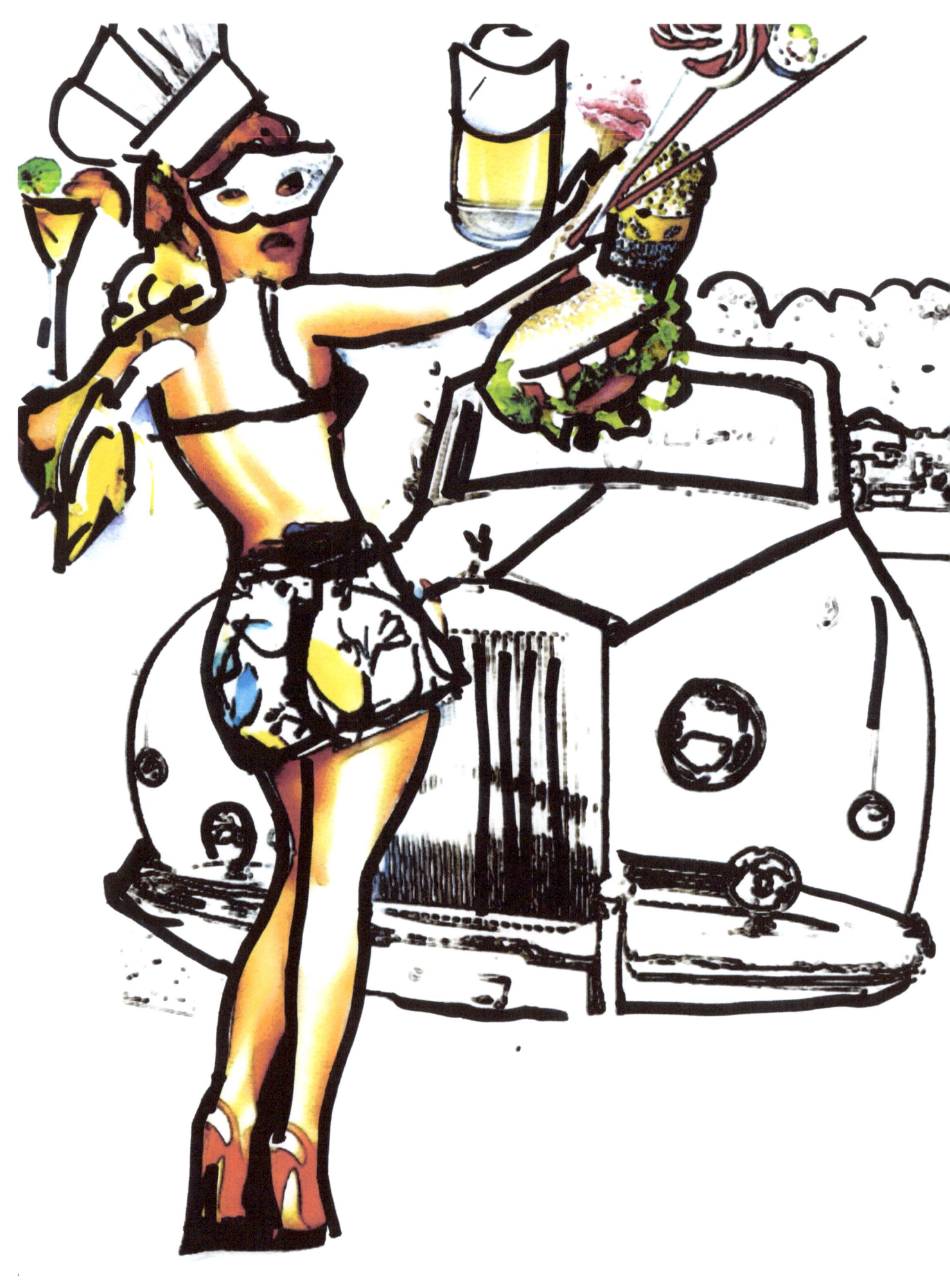

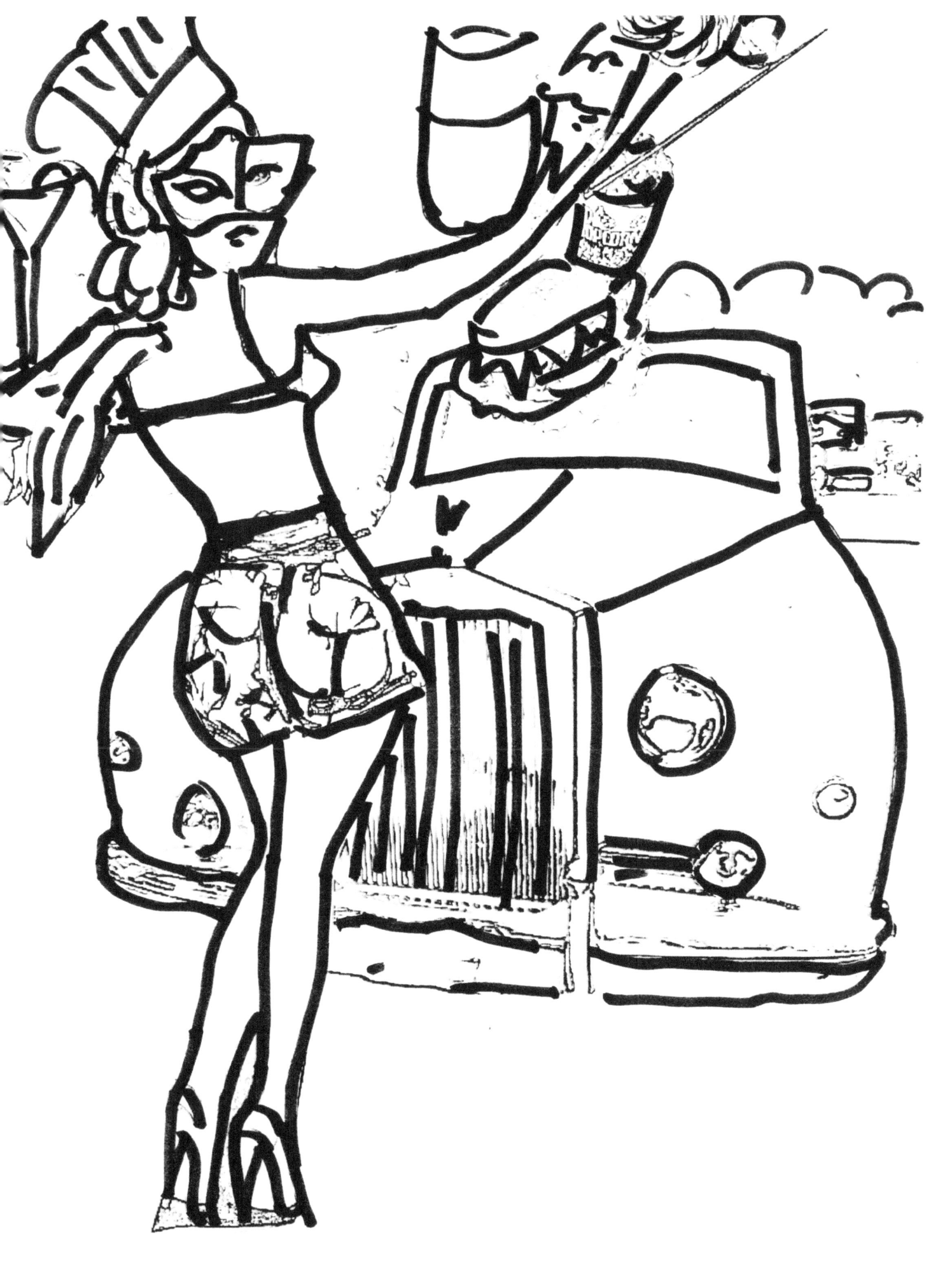

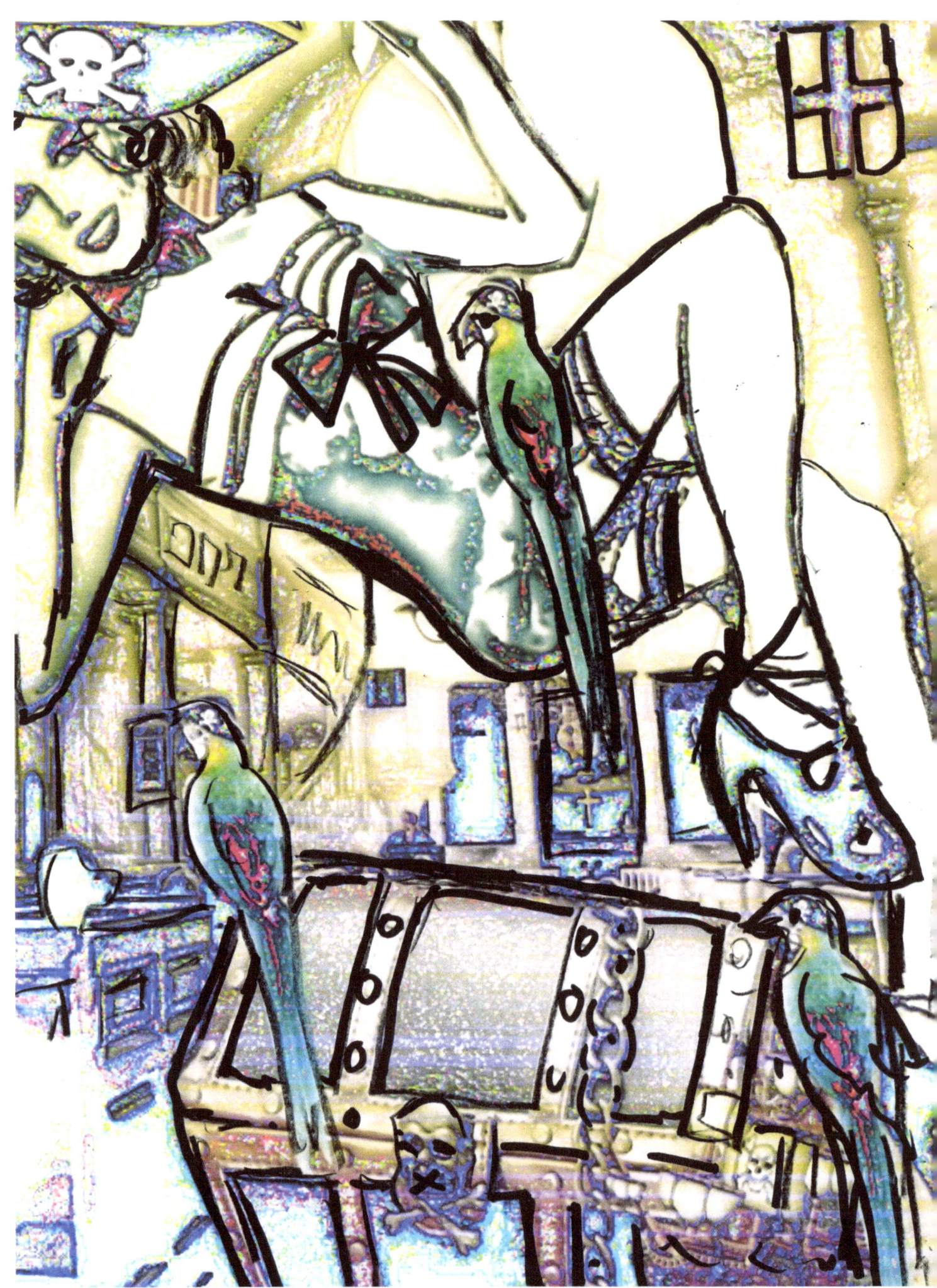

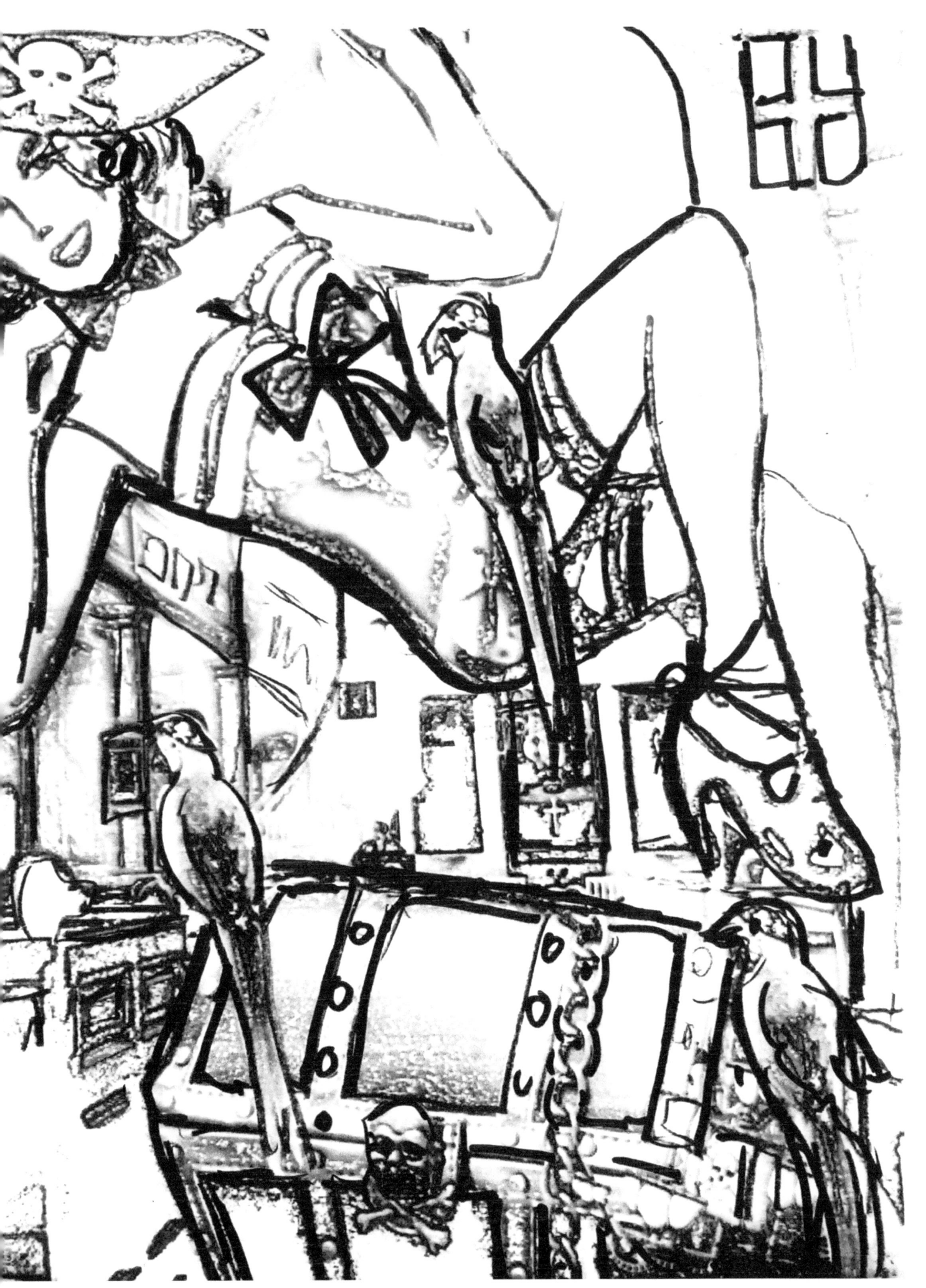

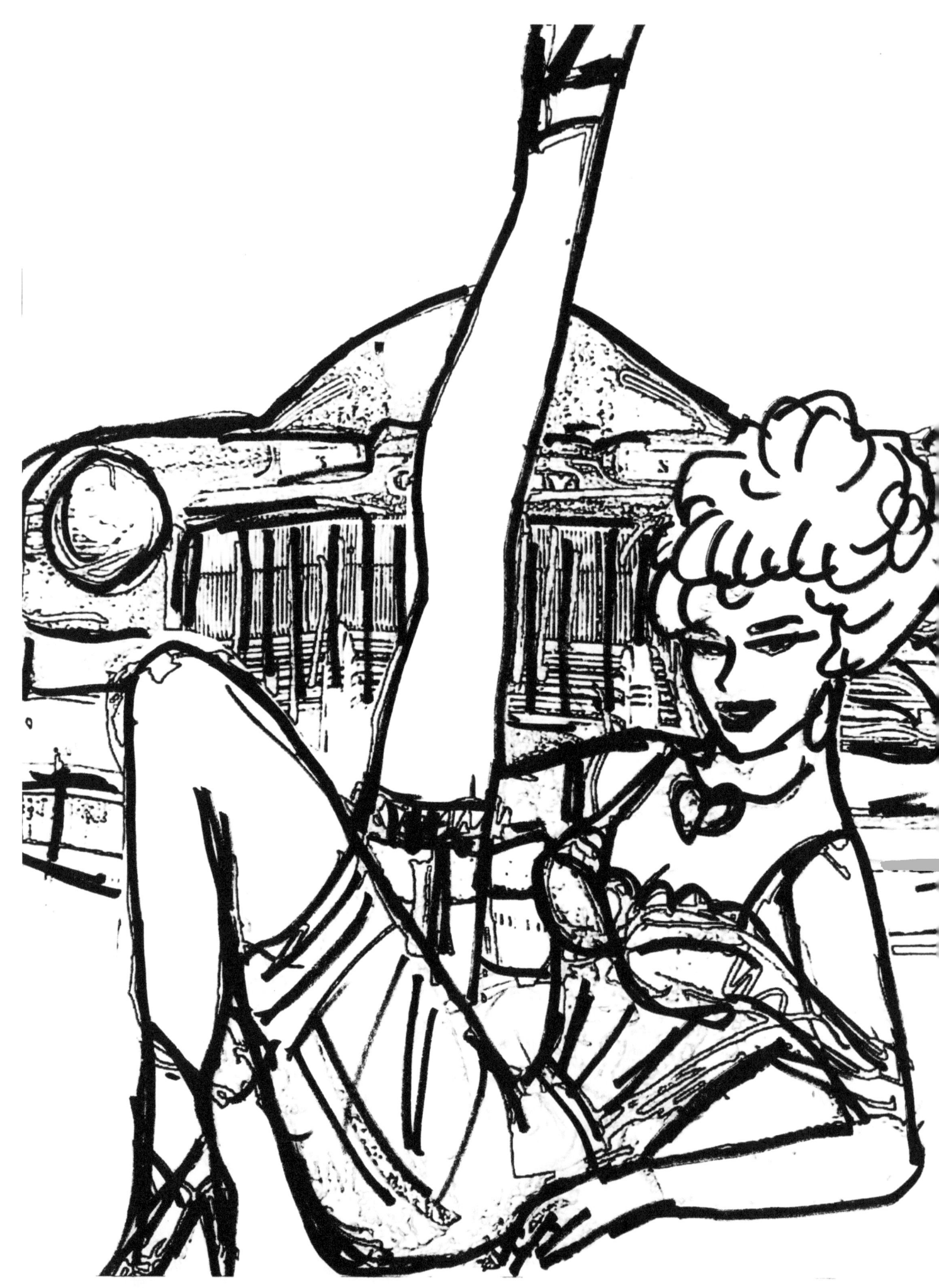

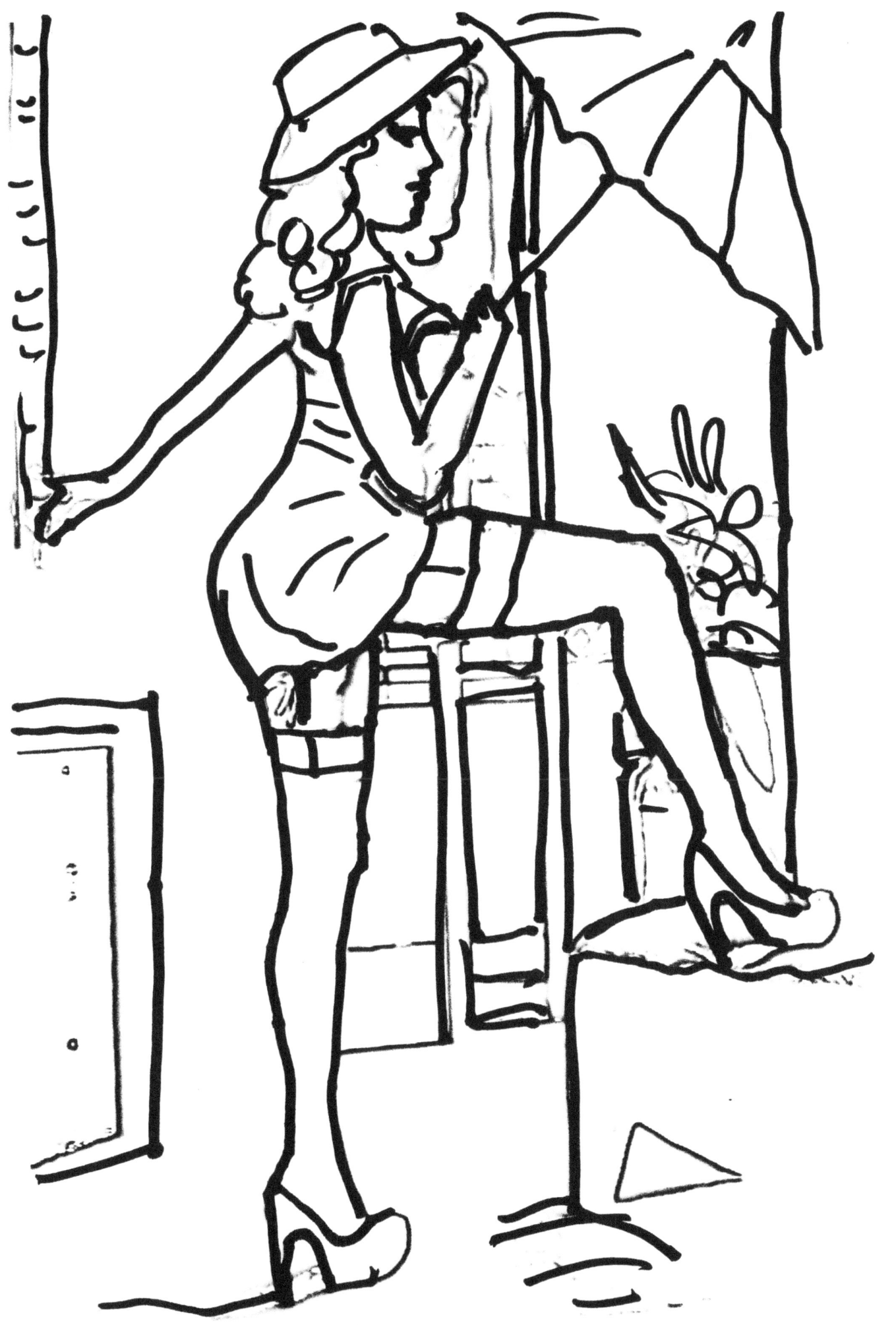

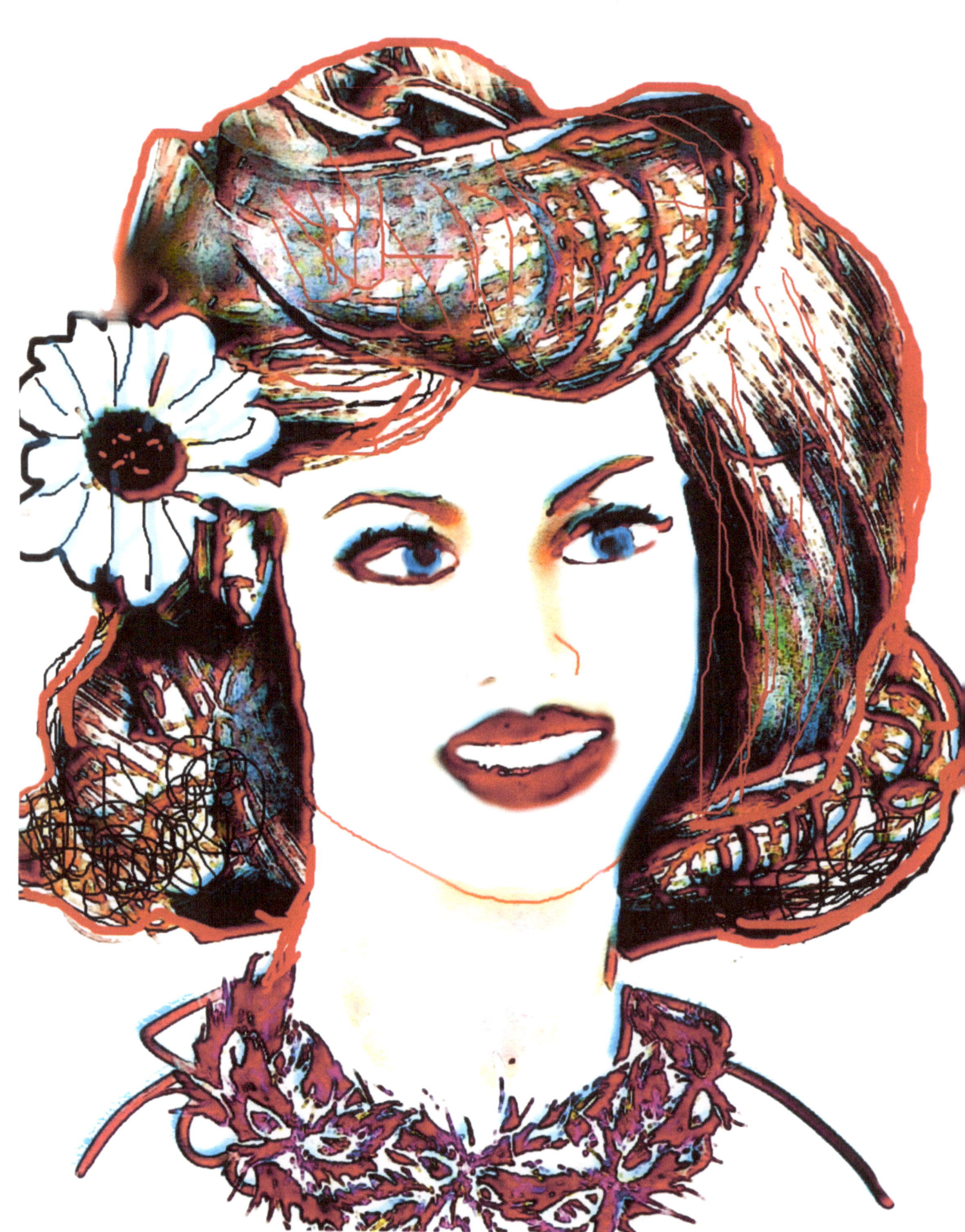

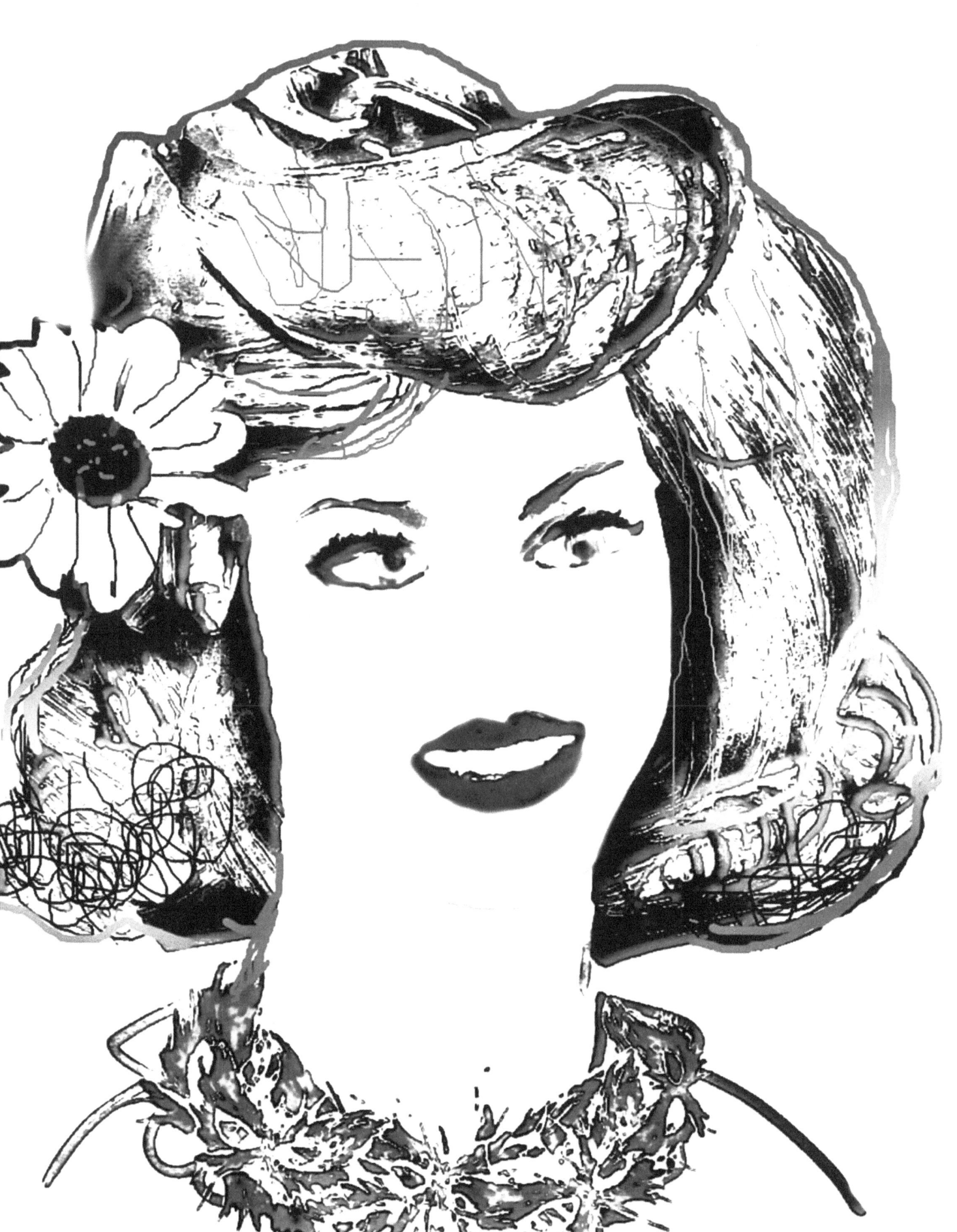

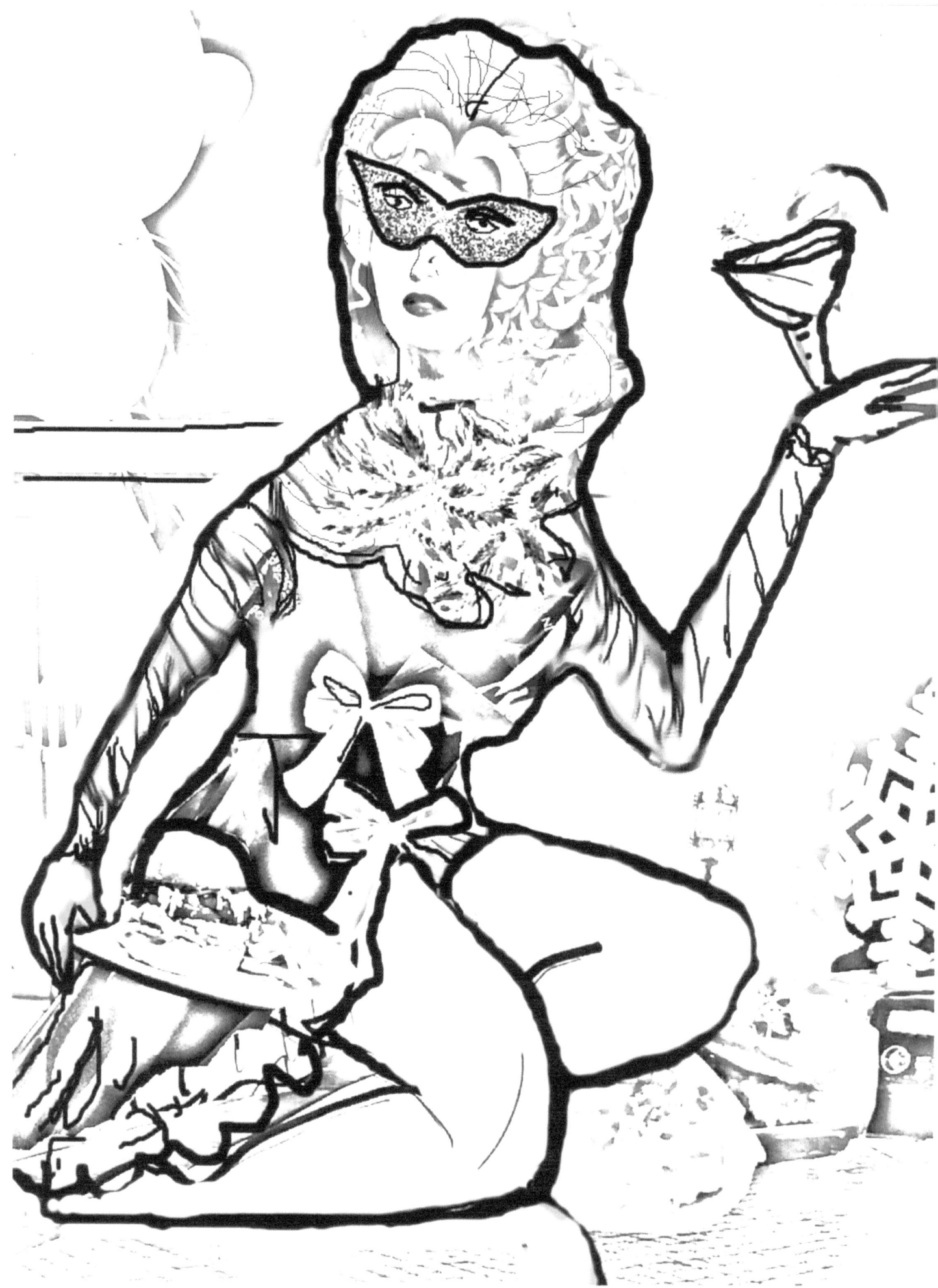

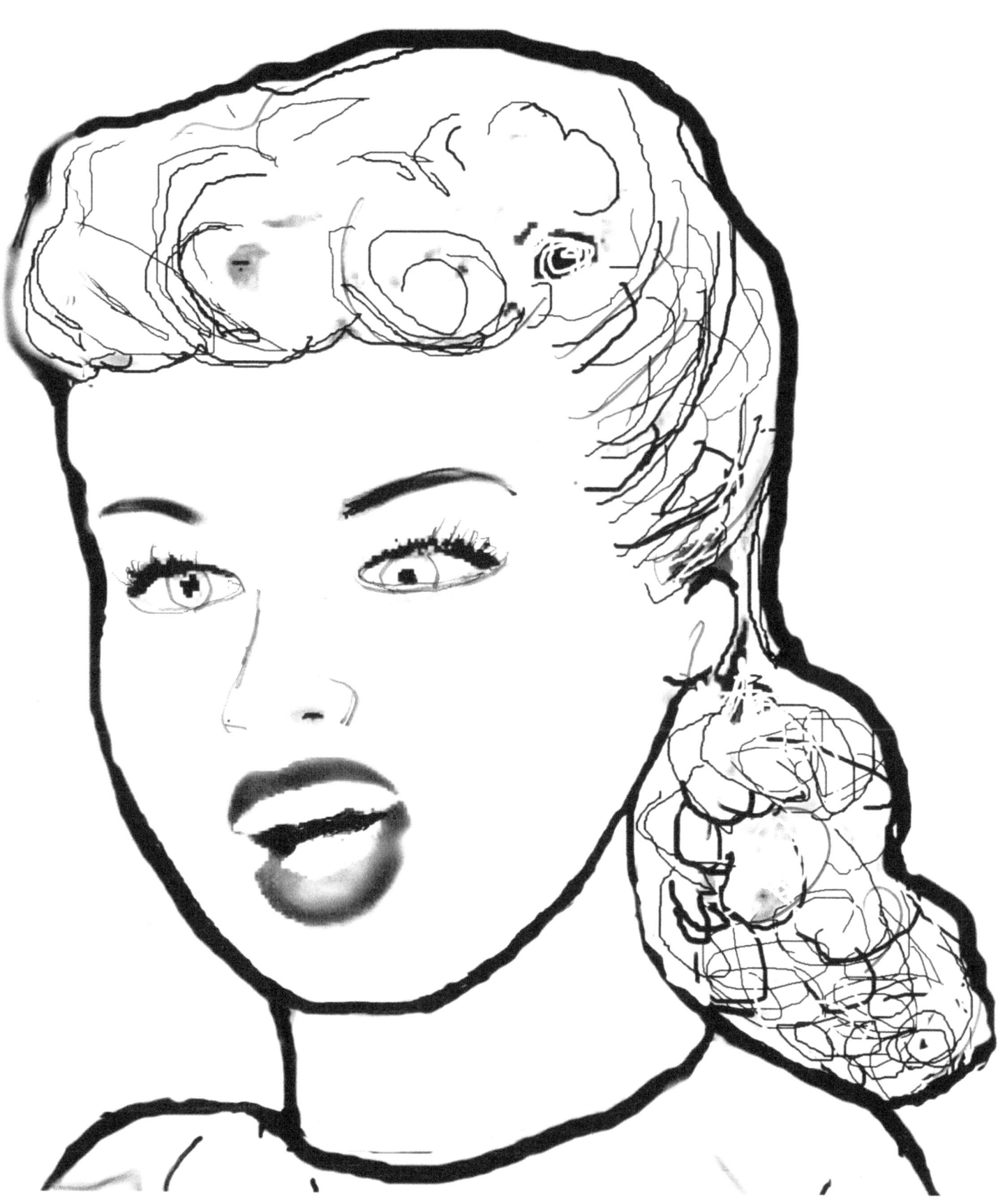

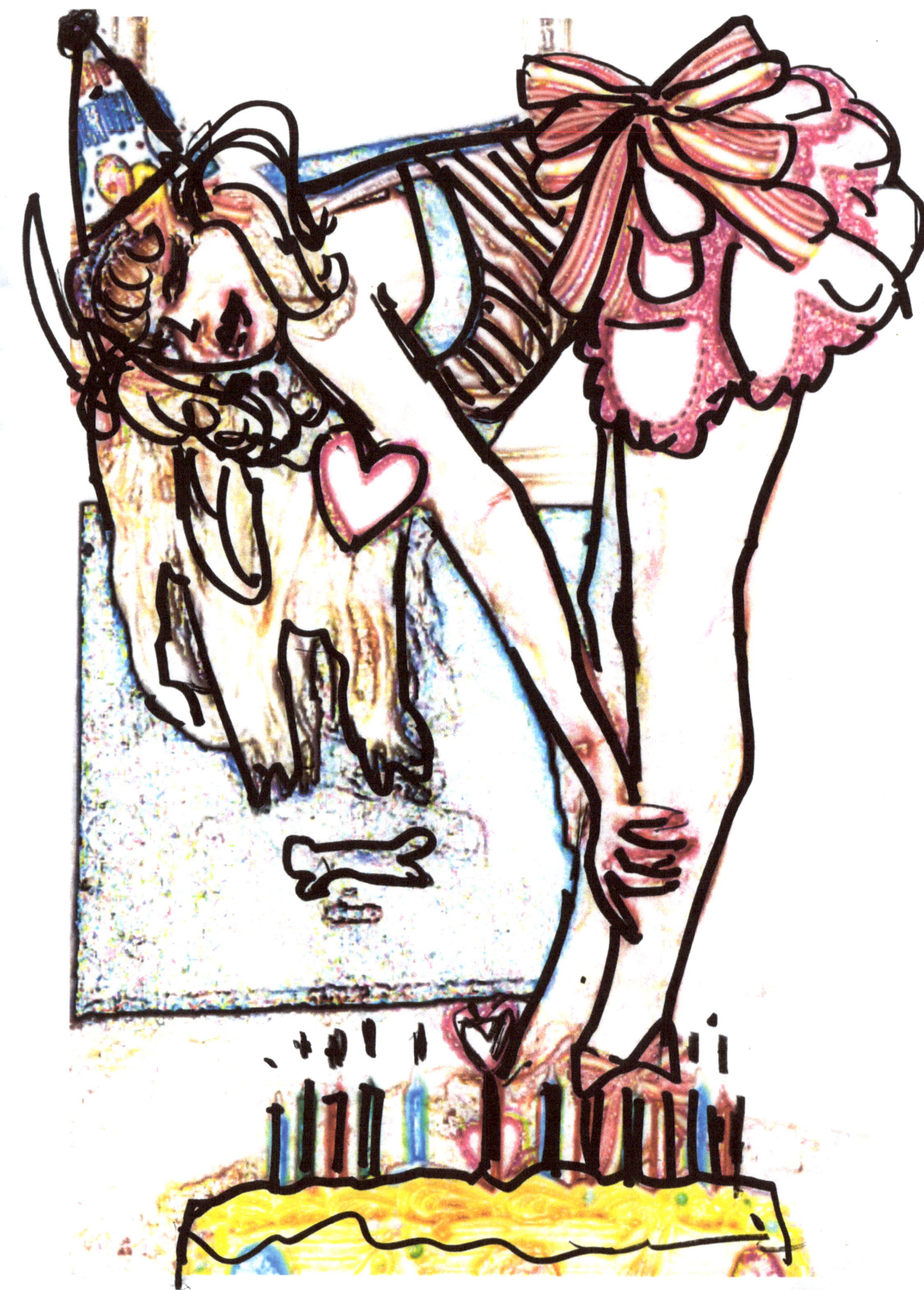

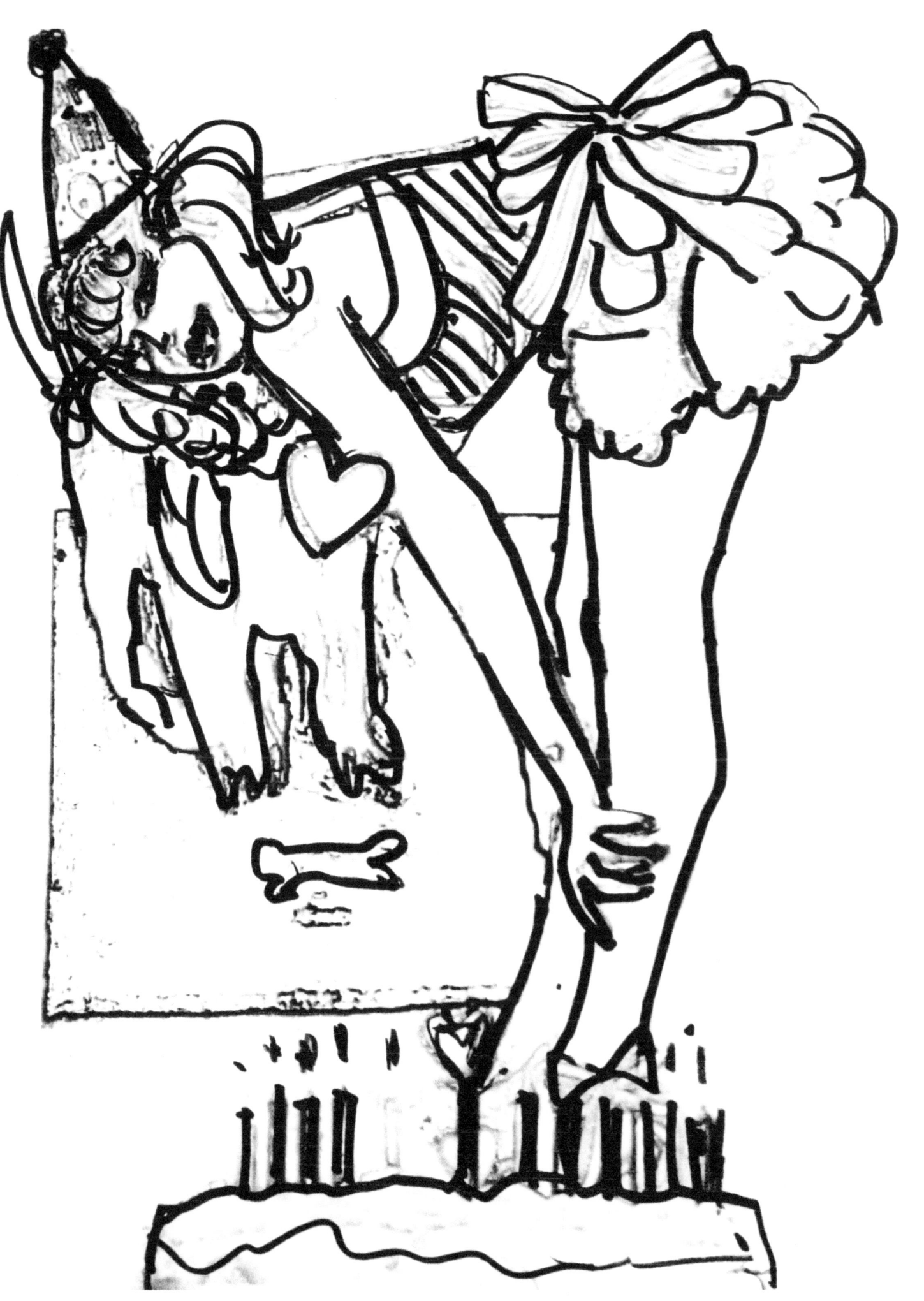

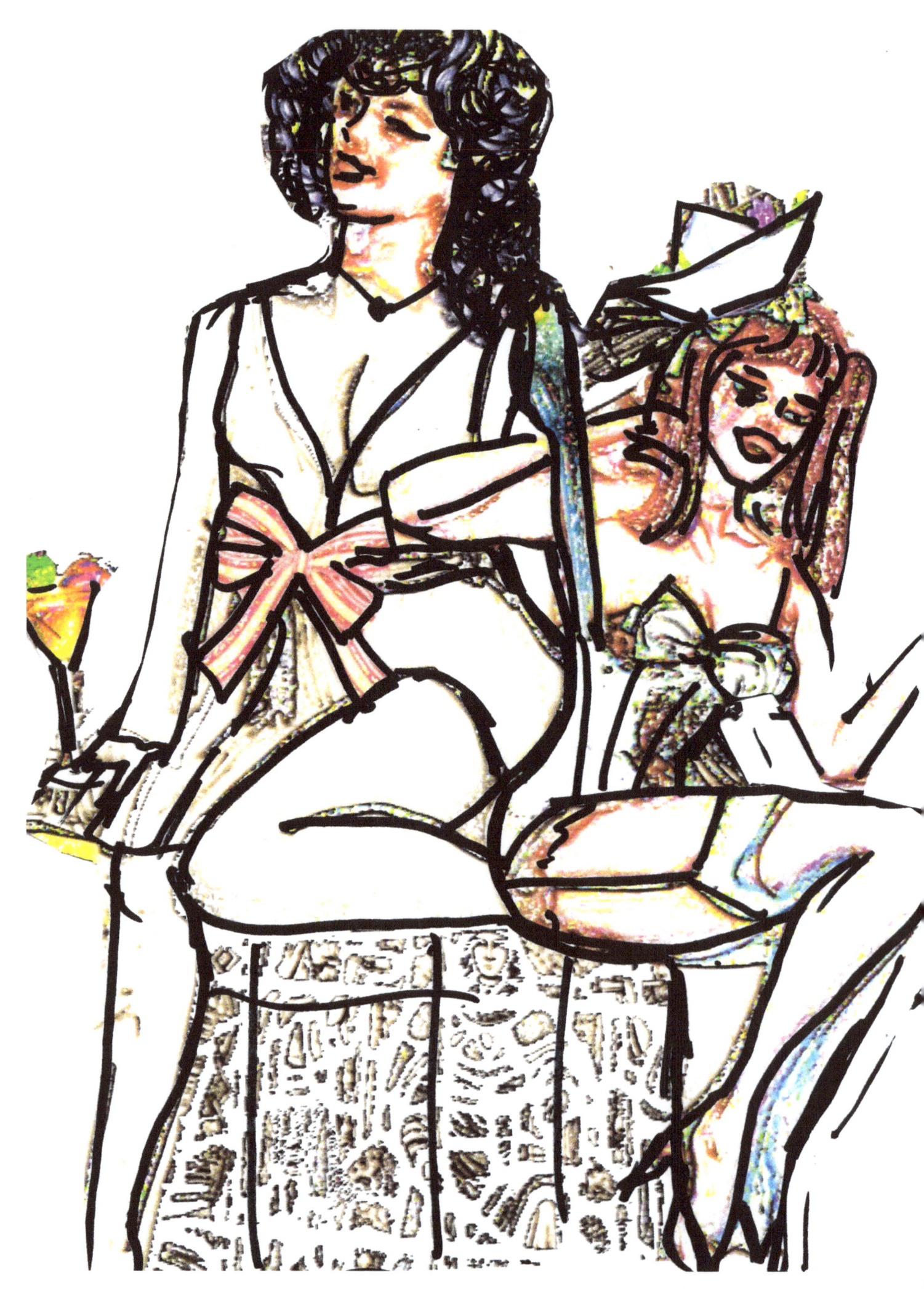

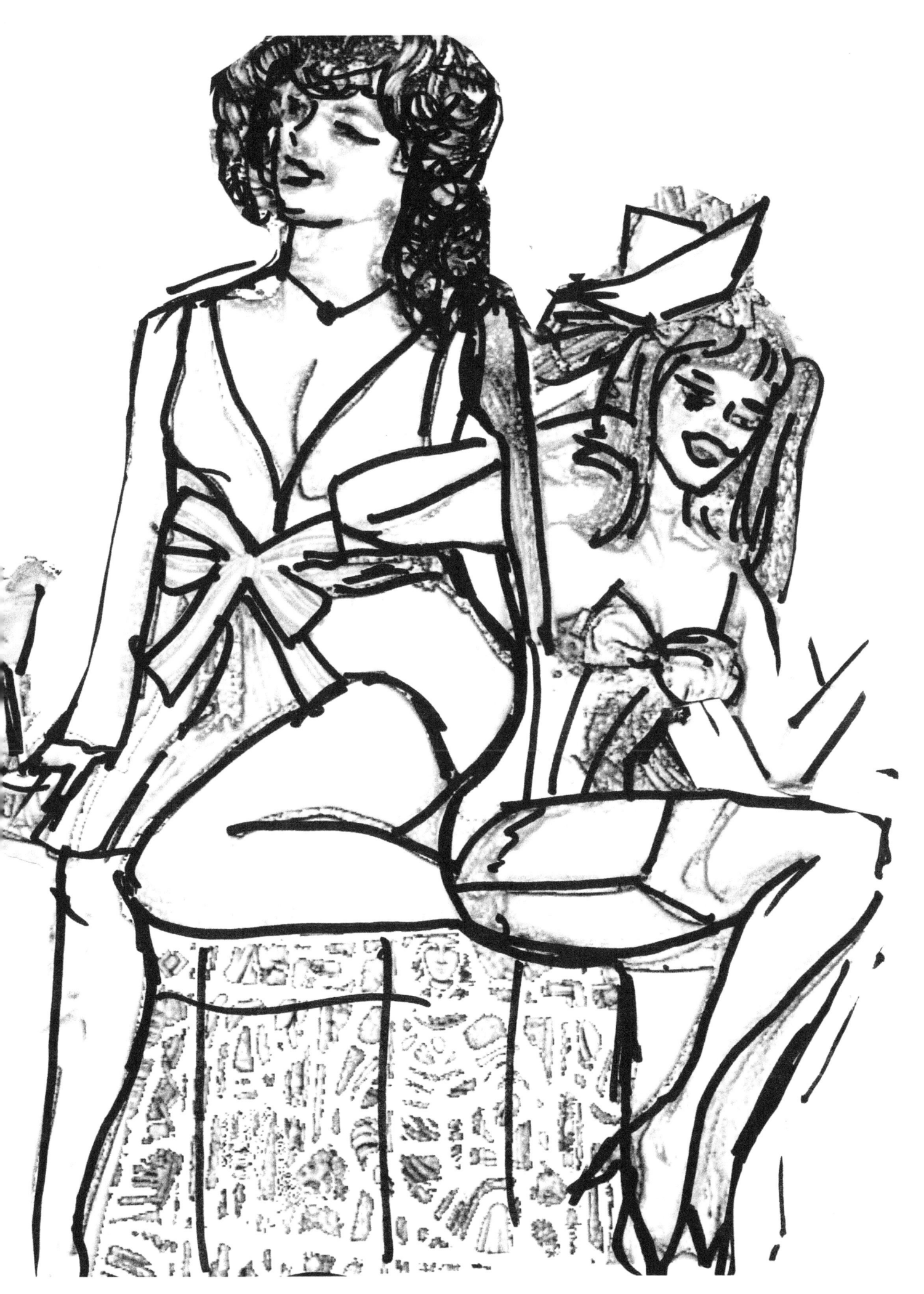

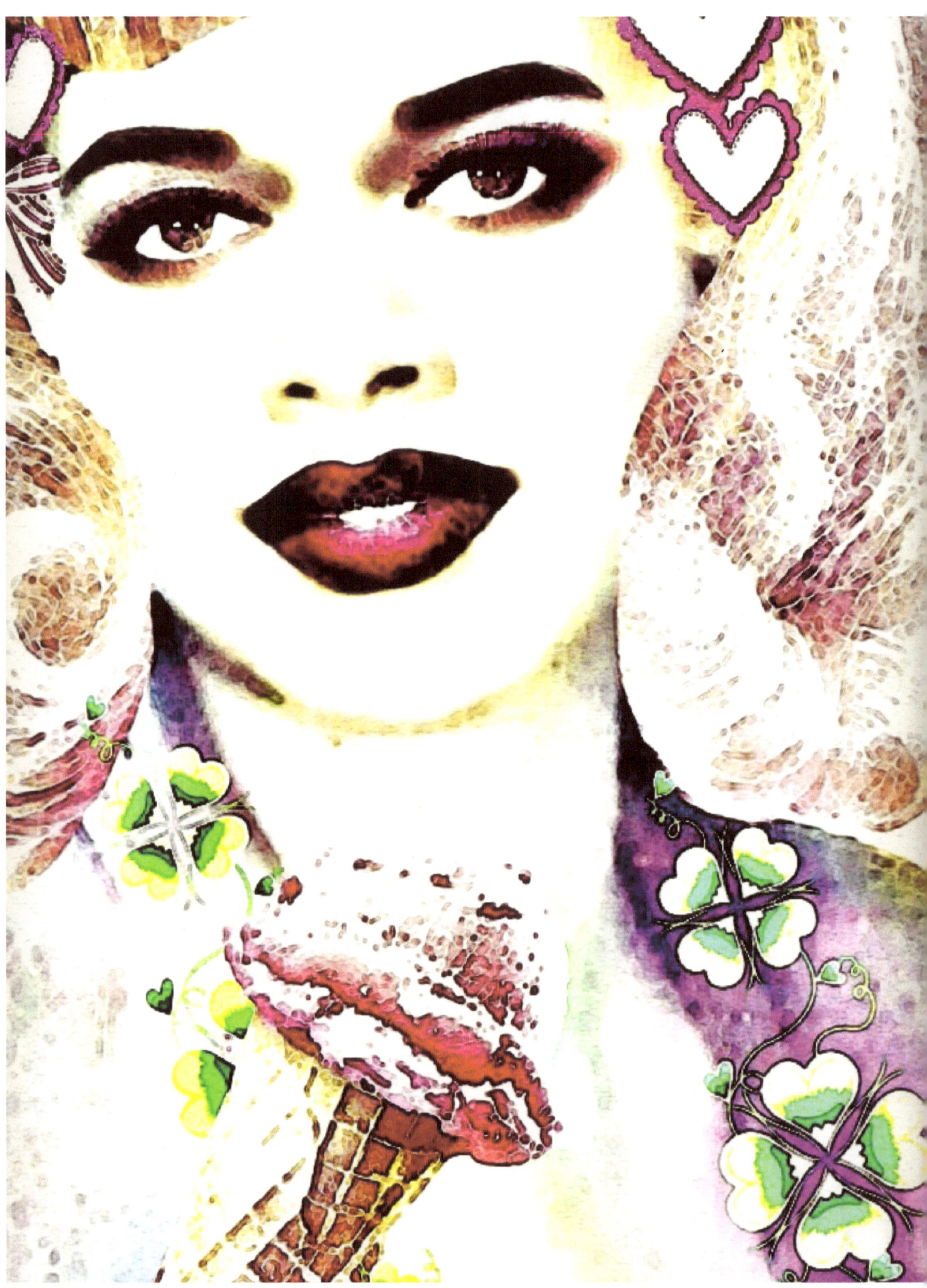

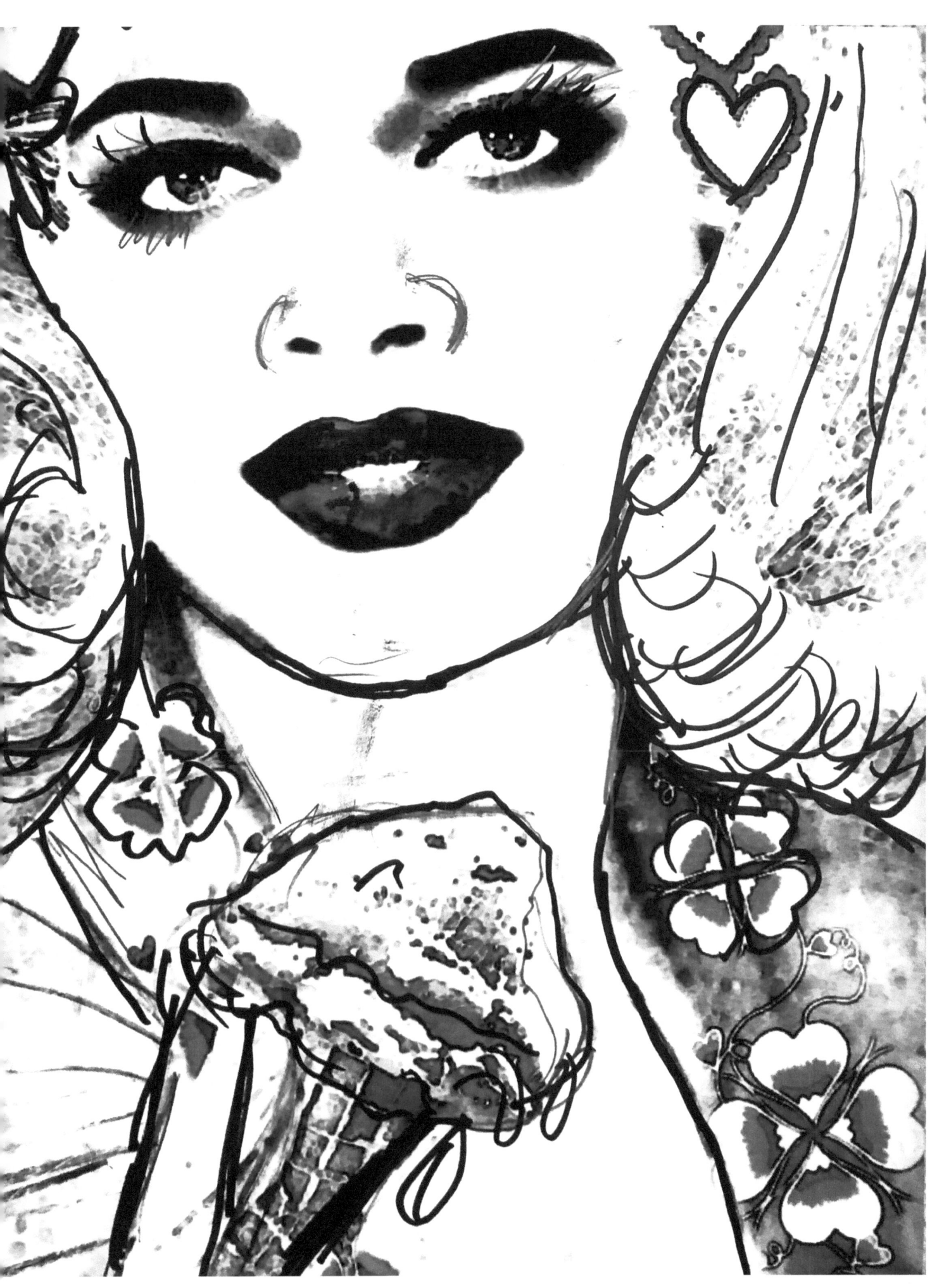

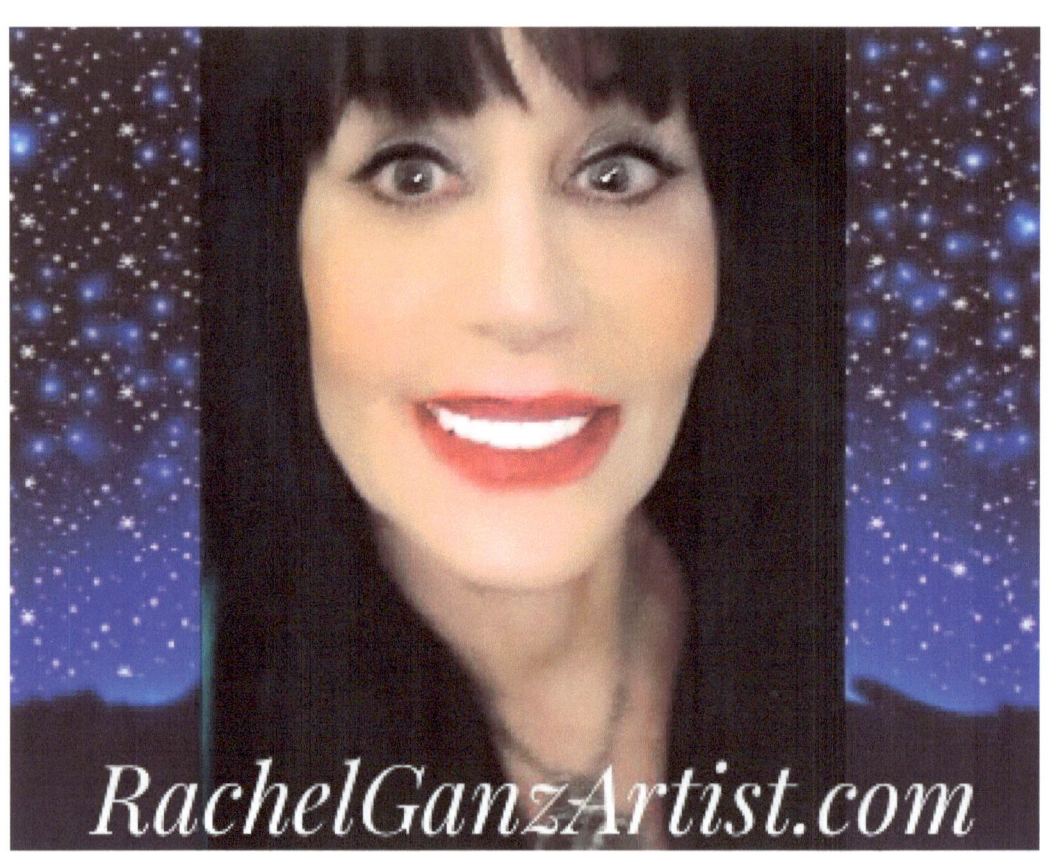
RachelGanzArtist.com